HOW IT FEELS
TO BE ATTACKED BY
A SHARK

edited by MICHELLE HAMER

also
SHOT IN THE HEAD
ABDUCTED BY ALIENS
CRUSHED BY AN AVALANCHE
AND OTHER TRUE STORIES

summersdale

HOW IT FEELS TO BE ATTACKED BY A SHARK

Edited by Michelle Hamer

First published in Australia by Thomas C. Lothian Pty Ltd in 2004

This edition published in 2005 by Summersdale Publishers Ltd.

Summersdale Publishers Ltd
46 West Street
Chichester
West Sussex
PO19 1RP
UK

www.summersdale.com

Printed and bound in Great Britain.

ISBN 1 84024 472 0

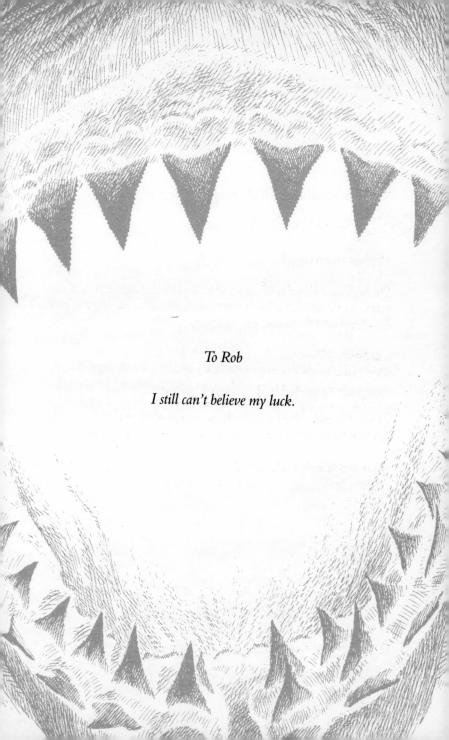

To Rob

I still can't believe my luck.

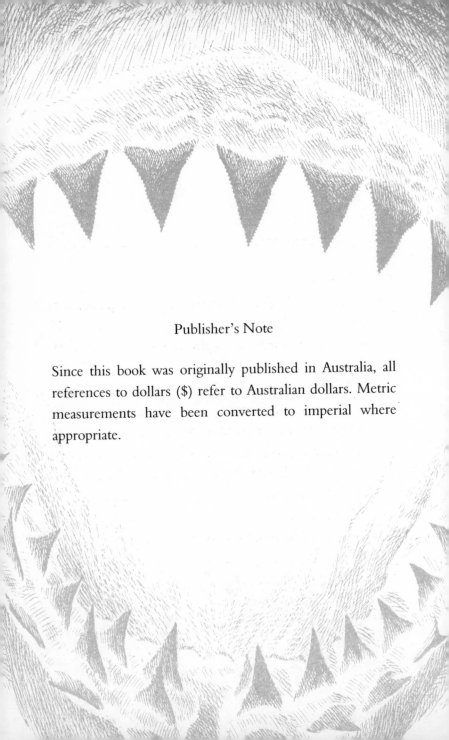

Publisher's Note

Since this book was originally published in Australia, all references to dollars ($) refer to Australian dollars. Metric measurements have been converted to imperial where appropriate.

Contents

Preface

I've heard so many stories this year – bizarre stories, heart-warming stories and some that have filled me with grief. Many left me breathless with tears or laughter, others were horrifying and some will never leave me.

There is a gamut of emotions and experiences within this book: all are true, all are told in the voice of the individuals who share them and all will touch you in some way.

I hope in reading this book you not only get the opportunity to gasp in awe and amazement, but also to sense some of the power of the human spirit as portrayed in these stories.

Many will echo in your mind for days to come, some will inspire you and all will provide an insight into the strength and resilience that come to people when the unthinkable actually does happen.

Michelle Hamer

Acknowledgements

It has been a privilege to step into the lives and hearts of so many courageous and positive Australians. This is your book, your stories, and I thank each of you for being so honest and open in sharing your story.

Thanks to Alice Ghent and Veronica Ridge at *The Age* newspaper, which ran the first *How It Feels* series that inspired this book.

Thank you to the beautiful Tracey Caulfield, who drove me to my first appointment with the publisher, helped me come up with great ideas, listened to me moan on bad days and babble on good days, cooked food for my kids when I ran out of puff, laughed at me when I decided to quit (every time!) and continued to be the best friend that she has been to me since we met at fifteen.

Harley, Ruby, Darcy and Oliver – I love you all. Dream big and don't let go.

Kell and Ads, thanks for your ideas and support. Love you both. To the future!

Thank you to Cathy Smith at Lothian Books for always being wonderfully positive and upbeat.

And lastly thanks co-publisher Geoff Slattery and Selwa Anthony, my agent.

How it feels to be attacked by a Great White shark

Allan Oppert, 46

I've been diving all my life. I love diving for crays. If the weather's good we dive once a week. I've seen sharks in the water before but it has never been a problem.

I'd been in twice that day and got some crays, but I thought I'd go back for these last three. I jumped in the water feet-first; normally I go in head-first but for some reason that time I didn't.

I stopped at about fifty-five feet (that's nearly seventeen metres) and as I'm looking at my depth gauge, I'm sort of in a standing position, just to let everything thicken up – my blood and so on.

As I'm studying my gauge I looked down below me and that's when I saw the Great White. I thought, 'Oh my God, here we go.' Straight off I thought, 'What a big shark!' Turns out he was about fifteen feet.

10

I wasn't worried at that stage. I concentrated on slowing my heart right down. As soon as I identified what it was, I thought, 'Well, a Great White, if it comes at me, he's going to try to knock me out,' because that's what they do – and he did exactly that.

I took a couple of deep breaths and relaxed and relaxed – because they can hear your heartbeats, these things – and I just thought, 'Well, if it comes, it comes, but I'll be ready.' And sure enough he spun around on the bottom and came straight at me. I took a deep breath and pushed my guts out. As he was coming up he just opened up his mouth and punched me with his nose. Then both my legs were in his mouth and there was just a huge force, a huge push.

It felt like my dive bottle was trying to come through my back because he was pushing me up to the surface with tremendous force. He hit me in the stomach with his nose, then he bit down, and I could feel the bite go in on top of my knees and underneath my calf muscles.

It was just excruciating pain. I thought, 'Hang on, he's going to bite my legs in half, my knees are going to snap.' The pressure was just unbelievable. I felt his teeth sink in and go right to the bone. I could feel his teeth grinding against my bones. My legs were in his mouth and he started thrashing me around like a rag doll – like a little fox terrier thrashing a rat.

It's the worst pain I've ever experienced – I couldn't wish that on anybody. That bite down on my knees and the bite at the back of my calf muscles – oh boy. You've got to remember that, in the bottom of its jaw, the Great White has two sets of teeth. When I felt his teeth hit my bone I thought he was going to break me. I was reaching for my knife to poke him in the eyes, but I think that as he came up, his teeth just sheared the knife off the side of my leg and then when he bit down I think he bit into my spear gun, which was lying across my lap. I'd put a new head on that spear gun and this thing was really sharp.

My mask had come off the side of my face, so I pushed it back on and I'm looking down and thinking, 'Whoa, what a big head.' His eyeballs were, I reckon, about thirty-five inches apart. He was twisting me around so much that I could see the gills just down below his eyes and I could count them all. This probably lasted ten seconds – or ten hours, I couldn't say.

He's got my legs in his mouth and I'm face-to-face with this massive head. I'm thinking, 'This is not happening, this is not happening, but yes, it's happening.' I knew I was going to die, but I didn't think it would be at that particular moment.

He let me go – he spat me out, I think. Once he'd bitten through the top of my knees he'd also bitten through my spear gun and bitten it in half, and three-quarters of it had gone down his gullet.

My theory is that my knife's inside him already – and it was a brand new knife too – and my spear gun's down there too, and he's probably thought, 'This is no good,' and he's let go.

By then my BCD is full of air. That's my buoyancy control device, which you wear as part of your vest, but I can't remember pushing the button to inflate it. It's compulsory when you're diving deep.

I'm getting pushed up to the surface. He's let me go and I've gone blasting straight out of the water; I've probably gone the last three or four metres just flat out. My mask had slipped down over my chin on the way up, so you can imagine the force.

When I got to the surface, that's when I thought I was going to die. As I got there, just knowing what these Great Whites do, I knew I had about ten seconds before he came back to finish me. I was counting, 'A thousand-and-one, a thousand-and-two…' waiting for him to come after me.

I yelled out to the boys on the boat to come and get me because I'd been attacked by a shark. I was screaming at them. As soon as they began to pull me into the boat the shark came up underneath me. One of my mates yelled out, 'Hurry up, hurry up, he's here! He's coming up!'

They pulled me in, and he came straight up underneath our boat and straight across to the other boat and attacked the propeller. He was pretty mad; he had a go at the anchor as well. He wasn't very happy at all.

My injuries were pretty horrific. I knew how bad they were because I'd probed with my fingers. I had to put my kneecap back together. It was sticking up in the air so I pushed my fingers in there and pushed it down. I could feel the muscles and tendons spilling out onto my legs. The pain was extreme; it was worse when I bound my legs up with an old fishing jersey and a towel. That's when my feet were starting to go numb.

It took us about forty minutes to get back in. I was lucky not to bleed to death. I could feel the blood running down and pooling around my buttocks. There was plenty of blood.

I was in hospital for six days and then it was about three weeks before I could walk again. I don't have any feeling in the back of my calves now and sometimes my knees seize up.

I've been back diving several times since, but not in that depth. I will though, because that's the only way to get the big crays and I love getting them. But I'm more wary now; I tend to look around a bit more carefully. I look into the distance as far as I can. I never used to have a care in the world under the water, but now I'm more aware.

How it feels to be struck by lightning – twice

Don Whitford, 57

I've become a bit of a standing joke because I worked for the Weather Bureau and I've been hit by lightning twice.

The first time was while I was working in Darwin. I was at football training and I went up for a mark at the goal post, and lightning hit the football. There was just a loud bang and it was quite frightening. I fumbled the ball and fell to the ground and we called training off.

It wasn't really a day of thunderstorms so it was very hard to pick where it came from; it just happened unexpectedly. There was this sudden flash that zapped across from somewhere and hit the ball, just as I tried to put my hands on it.

Funnily enough I didn't feel anything much, other than a tingling sensation, because of the fact that I wasn't earthed; I was up in the air. Somebody said I had a yellow

15

glow around my body as the lightning hit the ball, but I didn't see anything. It was quite extraordinary. The lightning probably hit the goal post and then arced across from the goal post to the ball.

Afterwards I felt a bit shaky, but I had no visible injury or pain. I could have been seriously injured if I was earthed because the charge would have gone right through my body.

I know that I was really very lucky. There're plenty of documented cases of people being severely injured, losing fingers and toes, or being killed. But we just laughed about it and thought no more about it really – it was all over in a flash – literally.

The second time was also in Darwin, about three or four years after the first time I was hit – and I really should have known better. I was running with a group called the Hash House Harriers, just a mob of blokes who got together to run during the week. This day the cloud base was about fifty feet from the ground. It was a really low, horrible, tropical thunderstorm with lightning and thunder and torrential rain. We were running across flat ground with water up around our ankles – that's how heavily it was raining.

There were about twenty of us or so, running across an open oval, up across a little rise, and we spread out to go around this little tree which had just been planted – it was no more than six and a half feet high – and then lightning struck. It arced out – we think it hit the tree – but it arced out and hit the water and just blew us all up in the air, all of us. That was rather frightening and painful.

Immediately it hit I knew what was happening and I just thought, 'You bloody idiot, what are we doing out in this?'

I just cursed our stupidity for being there and I honestly thought somebody was going to be dead.

I looked around and there were about twenty grown men in foetal positions on the ground, just lying still. It was quite horrifying. I thought: 'Oh God, somebody's going to be dead here,' but fortunately nobody was.

Four of us were quite badly off; we suffered burns and a bit of shock, and I had burnt feet because the charge going through the water boiled it and scalded our feet. It was like someone pouring a boiling kettle over your feet – the skin was red-raw for a while.

Somebody else had a big burn on his chest; another guy had a burn on the side of his head, and one guy stopped breathing for a while. An ambulance came and took four of us to hospital.

I've had a whiplash injury in my neck ever since then, which was from being thrown up in the air. I just remember being airborne for a second or two and it felt like somebody had hit me over the back of the neck with an iron bar. As the volts go through you, your whole body jars and you go into spasm, and your neck jolts back.

It wasn't till we left hospital that I thought about being struck twice and I decided: 'Well, strike three and I'm out; I'll have to be careful.'

I stayed in Darwin for another few years after that but after several more near misses, I made sure I got well out of it whenever there were storms around.

One particularly horrific time we were out prawning; we walked out into the water, dragging the prawn net behind us on the mud flats, when a storm came over and lightning was hitting the mud flats. Of course we were the tallest thing on the mud flats so we lay down in the mud, which was just lovely! Then it rained so much it was almost like the tide coming in. Then the mud crabs started to come up and we thought: 'This is like a horror movie,' because lightning was hitting the ground within 150 feet of us. Eventually we just ran and hid. I think I've pushed my luck a bit with lightning.

After all those incidents I became pretty wary of storms. One time in Darwin I was mowing the grass and a storm came over, but because of the noise of the mower I didn't hear it. All of a sudden there was a flash and a bang and I literally dropped everything and ran under the house in fear – it was just an automatic reaction. A few minutes later I felt like a real dill and looked around to see if anyone was watching. It must have looked funny, but I just don't take any chances these days.

How it feels to rescue a child from a flooded drain

Alan Sykes, 46

In 1996 we had three days of continuous torrential rain in Coffs Harbour, which resulted in severe flooding around the area.

I was a detective in the police force at the time. One morning my partner Gavin Dengate and I went back to the station after an early job. We were just grabbing a cup of tea when we heard the call come over the radio that there was a young boy lost, possibly trapped in a stormwater pipe.

We raced around to the people who had made the phone call. There was a guy there with two little blokes, and they were pretty traumatised. They had been playing in the flooded creek on their boogie boards, then were heading home when they turned around and realised this young guy who had been with them had just gone.

They realised he must have been swept into a stormwater drain, which was only about thirty-five inches wide and

19

in full flood. He wouldn't have been able to see anything because it would have become pitch dark very quickly.

This poor boy of only about eleven or twelve was washed with phenomenal force down this pipe and – who knows if it's divine intervention or not – the end of the pipe dips down at quite a severe angle and then goes into a grate, but somehow a piece of timber had become wedged across the pipe, just before that dip. In the pitch black he's hit this thing and grabbed it. He's there, it's freezing cold, a phenomenal force of water is pouring on top of him and all he can do for the next hour or so is just scream for his life.

We didn't know where he was, so we stripped off and pulled some cement covers from the drains, which allowed us to see down into the stormwater pipe. We thought we could see the boy or what we thought was his body because there was no sound, no movement. It was about 300-odd feet down the pipe. We thought if it was him we might be able to get him out and resuscitate him.

We didn't really have any equipment and we were working against time because there'd been so much rain, but in another case of divine intervention it had stopped raining by the time we got there.

Somebody brought a rope. It was a bit of a mental tussle between my partner and myself about who was to go in there, but I was the senior man and I said I was going in. If I had waited a second longer Gavin would have been straight in there. We're both dads with little kids.

They gave me the rope and I tied it around my waist and jumped in. The flood of water washed me down about sixty-five feet. I shouldn't have done that because I realised immediately that the rope was totally and completely inadequate and that it wouldn't hold me. The water was just so strong. I'm a pretty big guy, about six foot two and fifteen-odd stone but this water was just washing me around like a feather – it was incredible. I said, 'Stop this, get me out,' so they pulled me out.

By that stage the SES (State Emergency Services) had arrived. They gave us a proper lifeline rope. More cops had arrived. I said I'd go down and would tug on the rope three times if there was a problem. They gave me a torch, and I jumped in, lay prostrate and just let the water wash me down.

As it got darker I used the torch and realised that it wasn't the boy we'd seen, just debris stuck there. Then I realised I'd actually got myself stuck because the further I went down the drain, the more I backed the water up; I'd completely dammed myself in. I started to yank frantically on the rope, hoping that Gavin would understand. Fortunately he had realised what had happened and was in the pipe himself and yelling back to the surface to get every man and his dog to help pull me out.

It was a case of lying down and waiting for them to pull the rope back and trying to find a little air pocket every now and then to get a mouthful of air before going back underwater. I was just hoping like hell that the rope would hold. It was terrifying. I honestly thought I was going to drown, but also going through your mind is: 'Well, what if a kid is down here too, what's he going through?' You have a multitude of emotions and thoughts. It's pretty amazing actually because you feel quite matter-of-fact; you just think: 'This is it, I'm going to drown.'

I finally got to the surface and there were lots of police and SES and they said, 'Well, what do you reckon?' and I said: 'Well if he's down there we'll be looking for a body because there's no way he can survive that amount of water.' Unfortunately at that stage his mum had arrived, but I'm not sure if she heard me say that or not.

At the same time someone said they could hear a child screaming down the highway, so we jumped in the car and raced down there. There was traffic and people everywhere and you could hear this boy screaming and screaming, and everyone was running around like chooks with their heads cut off. Some were suggesting we get a JCB to dig the pipes up.

We looked into the manhole and the water was bubbling up into it so you couldn't see down where you wanted to go.

Somebody produced a ladder and Gavin went straight in and I went straight in after him. We got under the water and somehow popped up in a junction where six stormwater pipes met; a couple of them were flooded and just pouring water in on top of us, and somewhere in one of those pipes was this young boy. His screams were reverberating around the pipes, along with the roar of the water, and it was just the most unbelievable experience to know he was alive, but not know how we were going to find him and get him out.

We decided just to go up whatever pipe we could, but because we were going against the water it was terribly difficult. Gavin was crawling up his pipe and I went up mine and I thought I could hear the boy in mine, so I went back and got Gavin.

I'm trying to crawl up this pipe and, because it's so slimy and muddy, to try to get a grip on anything is almost impossible with the water pushing against me. The boy's still screaming out of control and I'm trying to scream out to him but it's just a waste of time. I was more or less dragging myself along with my fingernails and toenails and kept shining the torch ahead, and I think the boy must have seen some light, because he stopped screaming for just a short time. I got close enough to see him in the torchlight and I could tell that if he let go he'd come towards me, so I'm screaming, 'Let go, let go, come to me, come to me!' and he did.

He let go and was washed straight into my arms and I grabbed him. I said, 'Young man, you just say, "Thank you, God".' He said, 'Oh thank you, God.' I pushed him, and the water washed him down to the ambulance guy.

Up at the surface people were yelling, 'He's got him, he's got him.' His mum was there, she'd heard him screaming for his life. News footage shows this little drowned rat being hauled up the manhole. The ambulance crews put him in a space blanket and his mum threw herself on top of him and the crowd just went berserk.

I got out and went back to the car because I was physically and mentally exhausted. I was freezing cold, I just had my boxer shorts on and to this day I don't know why I took my slacks off to go down there. One paper had an absolutely wonderful photo of me standing on the edge of the highway with my boxer shorts on – it's not a good look.

I had blood and abrasions all over my back so the guys took me back to the station for a shower, and I just sat on the floor and bawled my eyes out.

Physically the boy was OK. He was very, very cold and in horrible shock, traumatised to the max.

I'd been a police officer for more than twenty years. I'd seen death and carnage on a regular basis and endured a lot of trauma, but this was an eleven-year-old child and his life was in the balance for so long; he had no way of knowing that help was coming.

He suffered horrendously when he went back to school; he had kids and even teachers saying, 'You should have drowned, you little bastard,' because he wasn't a great kid. He continues to suffer, I believe. I organised for him and his mum to go for crisis counselling for a while.

About twelve months before this I'd been involved in an incident where two police officers were murdered, so I'd just been getting over that when this happened. I had a complete breakdown after the rescue, which was the end of my police career.

Some time later it was announced that I was going to receive the Cross of Valour, Australia's highest bravery award. For me personally it was extremely beneficial because it gave me some sense that my actions were vindicated. I'd loved my police career and didn't want to leave. I was saddened that Gavin didn't get the same award because I felt he really deserved it. He got the Star of Courage, the second-highest award. We also each received a Galleghan award from the Royal Humane Society of New South Wales.

At the end of the day it's a great story because a child's life was saved – there can be no greater thing.

How it feels to lose a leg

John Eden, 48

" **I had a** motorcycle accident in New Zealand when I was nineteen. I was riding home from work and got into a slide going too fast on my bike and hit a power pole. I was lying on the ground with my leg wrapped up my back and my head resting on my foot and I thought: 'Oh no, my foot's not supposed to be there.'

I can't remember the next three weeks because I fell into a coma. Apparently I left this world a couple of times, but I can't remember any of it.

They reckon I broke almost every bone in my right leg from my hip to my big toe. My foot was crushed. It was all a bit of a mess.

It wasn't till I woke up and couldn't feel my legs that I realised I must have done something really bad. I was a rugby player and had just been picked for the junior All-Blacks.

26

All I could think about was not being able to play rugby any more. Then I was worried about not being able to work – because I was a farmer.

I had fluid in my lower spine, which stopped the feeling going into my legs. The doctors were giving me lumbar punctures – sticking big needles in the small of my back to try and draw the fluid out. They did that two or three times and it wasn't working. It was very, very painful. The first two they did without anaesthetic and had to hold me down. They did it again after six months and the next morning I woke up and felt pain in my legs because the fluid had dissipated. I was hoping I could become normal again, be able to run around and do the things I used to do.

After eleven and a half months in that hospital they sent me to an orthopaedic hospital to have an operation on my foot. They put a bone through my ankle to relieve all the pressure. My leg was plastered up to my hip but I had these pains in my groin and the glands were up, so I went to the doctor and told him I thought my foot was infected. He said, 'I don't think so, but we'll have a look.' So they cut the plaster off and it was just all rotten. My foot had basically rotted with gangrene.

My leg was off within an hour because the poison could have gone all through my body. They took it off just beneath the knee and I went back to hospital for about another month or so. I was just lying there looking at the stump, and thinking how painful it was and wondering what I was going to do with my life now, wondering what the artificial leg would be like and all that.

At that stage I got into drugs and alcohol because I was feeling really sorry for myself and couldn't play my sport, which I'd loved. I was always thinking: 'I need another joint, I need another drink.' I was heading in a bad direction.

The doctors sent me off to get an artificial leg made, and they just gave me a leg, and some walking sticks and said, 'There you go.' They didn't even teach me how to walk. I got to the door, hung my walking sticks up and tried to walk from there to the taxi and fell over three times. I got in the taxi and went down to the pub and that was my life for the next eighteen months. I didn't handle it at all well.

One day a guy came into the pub and he had both legs off. He said, 'You used to be a good sportsman; are you interested in trying out for the Paralympics in nine months?' and I said, 'No, not really.' He came back a few times and I just thought he was a pest. But I woke up one morning thinking: 'I'm just not getting anywhere.' I had a hangover and a shitty taste in my mouth, and it was rotten. So I rang this bloke up and nine months later I won New Zealand's first ever Paralympics gold medal for an amputee. I was a high jumper and did running and throwing. I started to realise that there was more to life than just drugs and alcohol and feeling sorry for myself. I went home and was a bit of a star – the papers and media were there and I was feeling pretty special.

In 1982 I came over to Australia because it has some of the best amputee runners in the world, and I thought this was a good place to compete and to try to make a life for myself.

I'd started playing rugby league in New Zealand, with just one leg, at senior reserve level. I tried to get into a Melbourne rugby club, but no one would take on a one-legged player. Finally Moorabbin gave me a shot in the fourth grade, their old men's team, but they complained that I played too hard for them, so they sent me up to third grade; then from third grade to second grade, and finally I started playing rugby for Moorabbin.

In 1984 I smashed my knee because I had no knee cap from the accident. I took my leg off after the game like I always did, to have a shower, and the stump just swelled up and never went down again, so they had to amputate it above the knee. That ended the rugby and the running.

Not having that knee there slows you down incredibly, but this time I accepted it a lot better. I got the best artificial leg I could and just got on with my life. I took up discus throwing and went to the Paralympics in 1988 in Seoul, and I've been an international athlete ever since.

I'm very passionate about coaching rugby now that I can't play at all. I spend a lot of time coaching athletics and rugby. I'm coaching nationally ranked athletes in the able-bodied field as well as the disabled field.

I've been to five Paralympics and have won medals at each one except Sydney. Since Seoul I've been ranked one, two or three in the world as a discus thrower – up to 2000 when I retired.

I won the discus world championships in 1994. Three days before I left, my fiancée, Mandy, got killed in a car accident.

I wasn't with her when she died. The cops came knocking on my door to tell me that she had died, and I had to tell her parents. Losing Mandy was the hardest thing I had to go through, harder than all my accidents. I think losing someone close to you is much worse than losing a limb. That was a pretty traumatic time. There've been a lot of downs in my life, but there've also been a lot of ups, and I think tragedy makes you more tolerant.

I wish I hadn't lost my leg but then I think: 'Well, what would I be doing if I hadn't?'

I'm pretty happy with my life at the moment. Since I lost my leg I've toured the world and I think perhaps I'm more of an understanding, compassionate sort of person; I was probably a bit arrogant before. I didn't know anything about people with disabilities. I was the national throws coach for the Paralympian team in Athens and I do motivational talks and visit schools. Life's pretty good.

How it feels to be 36 stone

Bobby Ballantyne, 42

I've made bad food choices all my life. I pretty much brought myself up, I fed myself and I did whatever I wanted. Dad was always big on veggies and fish, which I hated, so I'd make myself three or four big, thickly sliced toasted sandwiches, then go to the shop for ice cream, lollies or chips. I'd ditch Dad's healthy food in a hole out the back.

I was always a very solid girl and I got bigger after I started having children. I've got seven kids. I got bigger and bigger with each pregnancy. At first, though I weighed a lot and looked huge, I could still do what I wanted to do. I wasn't happy with the way I looked, but I could still do things.

But one day I couldn't climb on a chair to clean the top of the fridge, so I just didn't do it. The heavier I got the more things there were that I couldn't do, and it really

31

started to get to me. I had bad depression. When my weight went over 31 stone was the worst time.

I couldn't eat when I was depressed or worried. I'd have to think happy thoughts to get in a tranquil frame of mind, just enough to be able to eat.

I never ate breakfast, but by late morning I'd have at least half-a-dozen pieces of toast with heaps of butter and grilled cheese; then I'd start on my block of chocolate. If there was cake in the house I'd start on that as well.

I'd make myself a cup of tea, open a pack of biscuits and drain the cup without putting my mouth to it – just one biscuit after the other dunked in the tea. I'd eat until the packet was gone. I'd hide food from the kids because I didn't want to share it – it might have been a mud cake or whatever. I would cut off big pieces and shove them in my mouth as if I was in a race. I'd eat fast so I didn't have to share.

Night-time was my worst time for eating; I'd have my meal and then sit down to watch TV with whatever food I needed. When it was gone I'd get one of the kids to get me more chips, lollies or chocolates.

It wasn't just the quantities I ate that was so bad, but the fact that the food was full of fat and sugar – the worst garbage you can find on the face of the earth.

I kept eating and getting bigger, and in my last pregnancy the scales couldn't weigh me, but I think I was probably about 27 stone by the time I gave birth. The doctors told me I shouldn't have any more children, that it would be an absolute danger to my life. But I still didn't do anything.

There were nights when I would have really bad chest pains and I'd think I was going to die. I'd write letters to my children telling them how sorry I was, that I didn't mean to be like this. I'd make deals with God like: 'If you let me wake up in the morning I'll do anything – I will go on a diet, I'll lose the weight.'

I'd gone to bed really scared, but I'd wake up the next morning and there'd be no chest pains, which made me happy, and I'd go and eat. I'd look at my kids and think: 'I would do anything for you, anything,' but I didn't do that one thing.

I could walk, but not far. If I had to check the letterbox I would be totally exhausted halfway to the gate. I thought: 'That's it, Bobby, you're going to die, you're going to drop dead.'

I couldn't buy clothes. I had to wear ugly things just because they fitted me. I had a friend who made me skirts and tops that were basically tents. I chose horrible dark colours, because I thought they made me looked thinner. I couldn't wear knickers because there were none in my size. I bought super-size bike shorts and wore them as knickers to stop the chafing. I couldn't wear shoes because my feet and ankles were so swollen all the time – I had to wear sandals. I always felt totally ugly.

I slept in a chair in the lounge room for ten years because I couldn't lie down. I thought if I did I might die; the weight would all go up to my throat and I'd think I was going to choke. My husband bought me a recliner and I slept there.

I tried many times to get back into a bed but it was impossible. I couldn't turn over, I couldn't move. I went through five chairs in ten years; I broke them all eventually.

I've been sleeping in a bed for the past year now. I love going to bed – it's the best part of my day. It's one of the many magnificent feelings about losing weight.

I pretended not to be embarrassed about my weight. I became quite a rude person so that people would concentrate more on my rudeness than my weight. I was stared at all the time; friends would nudge friends and you could hear what they were saying. I was very embarrassed for my children; I knew what they must be copping at school.

People would talk to me loudly and slowly. The perception is that if you're big, you're stupid.

Chairs terrified me. They were my worst enemy – you could break them and end up on your bum, or you might not fit into them, or God forbid they could have arms or be made of plastic. If I was invited out for lunch, I would get my son to check out the chairs, how far I had to walk and if there were any stairs. If there were stairs I wouldn't go, unless the seats were solid wood without arms I wouldn't go. It was a life of restrictions.

About eighteen months before I started to do something about my weight, I was diagnosed with type-two diabetes; it didn't mean anything to me though. I probably spent the next year eating more chocolate and sweets than I ever had. I did start to think more about it though, and it began to scare me.

The big crunch came one day when I was having a shower and I slipped. It was a feat to get in there in the first place. I was really, really scared – there was no way I could get up.

I called for my son; he came in, took one look and started crying. I said, 'The fire brigade will have to come and take out the wall.' He said, 'Please, Mum, just try to get up.'

So much was going through my mind, like: 'How can you do this to your children? This beautiful young man just destroyed.' I was scared for the kids; that it was going to be on the news.

I sent my son to get every pillow he could find and we lined the bath with them. He had to get a pillow under me but the sheer strength I needed to raise my own weight was huge – even for one second it was torture. Finally he did it, and I was laughing and crying. Then I had to get onto my knees; I can't really describe the pain of that – I've never had a big truck sitting on top of me, but that's kind of how it felt, it was absolute agony.

But I did get onto my knees. Grabbing hold of the sliding door, I got there. I was crying harder and harder. My son ran and got a kitchen chair and I used it to lever myself up. He sat on the chair and I had to lift 36 stone. By some miracle I did it. It was one mighty heave. My son was cheering.

And that was it for me – it wasn't the agony of getting up or the risk of the fire brigade – it was my son and my daughters.

My daughter and I joined Weight Watchers but they couldn't weigh me because their scales only went up to 30 stone. I had to be weighed in a back room on old-fashioned scales. What depressed me was being told I had to lose twenty-four and a half stone, the weight of several entire people. I started to worry that I couldn't do it.

Then they told me that when I lost eleven pounds I'd get a bookmark; it was my first goal. I wanted that bookmark. I did my first week and pretty much from the start I got rid of the bad foods.

I lost almost eleven pounds in the first week; that spurred me on. I lost eight the second week. I just kept setting little goals for myself. My biggest goal was to get off the old-style scales and be weighed like a normal person.

In the past eighteen months, I've lost 21 stone and counting. My goal weight is eleven and a half stone and it's well and truly within sight.

How it feels to be caught in an avalanche

Mike Balfe, 44

I went to Alaska with a group of friends who were all serious skiers. On this particular day it was bright and sunny and hadn't snowed for about three weeks. The guides who were leading us were searching for untracked snow, because that's the whole reason you're up there. You go to Alaska basically to experience powder skiing.

In Alaska you only ever ski one at a time and the guide usually goes first. We arrived at the top of the slope that our guy had chosen for us and he was a little bit suspicious. He ended up digging a pit of some description to test the stability of the snow. I'd never seen this done before.

He felt that there was something not quite right, so he dug this pit, which would have been about four feet deep, and then he carved out a number of blocks of snow to check whether there were any sheer layers near the top.

He did a test where he tapped ice crystals onto a mirror to study their shape.

He decided it looked OK; if he thought it wasn't right he would have called the helicopter in and we would have been lifted to another slope.

In Alaska the slope is very steep and it then either plateaus out or ends up on a glacier but where the slope meets the glacier there is often a deep ice crevasse. We were to ski down about eight hundred feet and end up on a glacier. You don't go to Alaska unless you're an extremely competent skier. You're really out there and accidents do happen.

Anyway the guide went down and after about two turns he's vanished, you can't actually see him any longer because the slope is so steep. He comes out onto the glacier and radios back up to say, 'The skiing is fine; conditions are good.'

I skied down and chose to go basically where the guide had gone, so for the first four or five turns I'm looking to line up where I'm going to cross the crevasse over a snow bridge. Then I start into the run proper and when I'm halfway through a turn I see in my peripheral vision that the entire slope that I'm on has given way. I can see a crack forming and then it opened up behind me – probably only about fifty feet behind me. The entire slope that I am on is moving and I'm fifty feet into it, so there's another 650 feet below me that is moving – that's the good bit, but I wasn't thinking that at the time. I shat myself. I was very fearful and believed my life was in danger.

As I pressed back down into the snow, my downhill ski was removed by the movement of the snow, so I was on one leg.

I tried to go straight to get out of the area, but there was no way that was going to happen – on one ski I wasn't travelling fast enough to outrun it.

I got knocked off my feet and it surprised me how lucid you can be at that precise moment when you know you are in danger. My life didn't flash before my eyes like the cliché says it does, but I did think of my family – that was the first thing that popped into my mind. Then the thing I was concerned about was the crevasse at the bottom of the slope. I attempted to cartwheel and stay above the snow, so I didn't get sucked in and get buried.

I succeeded in staying on top of the snow and somersaulted, attempting to stay as tall as I could. I was all arms and legs, trying to hand-spring – not that I'm an acrobat or anything. I don't know how many times I flipped over – it could have been fifteen, it could have been twenty-five; I know it was a lot.

So I'm plunging down this hill and my only thought is to avoid going straight into the crevasse, that I should try to flip over the crevasse – not that I had any concept of where I was because I think I shut my eyes.

The guide was the only one who could see this happening and according to him I did a back-flip over the crevasse and landed quite heavily on my back. That took most of the momentum out of my fall and I think I flipped over twice more and ended up on my feet, facing up the hill. My equipment was all over the place; it was just me standing there with my backpack on and feeling very thankful.

I was in shock; I was shaking like a leaf. The guide was yelling at me to ask if I was OK and I put my arm up and waved because I couldn't talk, I was so winded.

The guide had radioed the helicopter and it was on its way and they put me in it and sent me home to the lodge.

I was extremely bruised and battered but that was all. I was very lucky not to have any other injuries. We took the next day off, but I skied for three days after that.

Now when I think back on it, it still disturbs me. I'd never given avalanches any credence, so to speak, I'd never worried about them. I've skied in many, many places that potentially could have been very dangerous but I never really worried.

I always thought I was good enough to ski out of it or get away from it. Well, I don't think that way any more and I will be a lot more circumspect going into untracked terrain.

How it feels to save a life on your wedding day

Jodiann, 38

66 **Simon and I** had known each other for only a few months when he proposed to me. The first time we met it was only for about twenty minutes; then it was three months before I saw him again.

He turned up on a motorbike; I waited all day for him.

I walked up and planted a kiss on his lips and we were engaged two days later – it was very quick. Less than six months later we got married.

I had only recently moved to Perth after working in Kalgoorlie as an emergency nurse.

We had both always wanted a really romantic, beautiful wedding. Our wedding cost a fortune; we planned a huge thing. We had an enormous marquee set up on a local peninsula and we were to go by boat from the garden where we got married, up the river to where

41

the reception was going to be held under a huge tree covered with fairy lights.

It was absolutely beautiful.

I had a Scarlet O'Hara-style dress with a heavily beaded bodice, very tight waist, massive hoops and a really long train.

The ceremony went well, but the second I got in the car to go to the boat I said, 'Let's skip the boat and go straight to the reception.' I had a definite feeling that something wasn't right.

But Simon said, 'We can't do that. John has been waiting for ages to boat the bridal party to the reception.' He was our best friend's father and was thrilled to have a role in our wedding. He was sixty and a dear friend. I felt strange and said again, 'I don't want to go to the boat,' but it was already organised.

We got on the boat and set off; there were two bridesmaids and two groomsmen, as well as John's wife, son and daughter.

We had only just got underway. I had snapped a suspender at the back of my leg and one of the bridesmaids was literally up my skirt trying to fix it; my leg was up in the air. Everyone else was getting their champagne organised.

I was the only one looking at John, the skipper. All of a sudden I saw that he went very grey, and with that he just salivated really badly and collapsed onto the throttle lever so that the boat went flat out, head first into the canal wall, and sent us all flying.

My bridesmaid was jolted up my body because she was still under my skirt; she ended up almost in my bra. We all fell backwards as the boat jammed into the wall. Everyone screamed. John collapsed. He had no pulse, no nothing – he was just dead.

I started resuscitating him. One of the groomsmen grabbed me and said, 'You don't get involved, it's your wedding day!' and I said, 'I'm the accident and emergency nurse, I have to get involved!'

All the guys picked John up and laid him flat in front of me. They had to move stuff out of the way so he could lie flat on the bottom of the boat. I said, 'I need this here, and this moved,' and everyone just did it.

There was chaos initially and then everyone was calm and they sat down. All I could think was, 'I have to save this guy.'

I picked up the hoops of my wedding dress and straddled him to do mouth-to-mouth.

His daughter dived overboard in her lovely wedding frock to swim up the canal to get help. His son grabbed the controls of the boat and pulled us away from the wall and kept the boat still so I could work on his dad.

All of a sudden John's heart just started beating by itself.

I was about to start heart compressions when he slowly came back. He had hardly any pulse, but then it got stronger and then he came back to consciousness. It was just amazing. It can only have been divine intervention.

I turned him on his side and his colour came back. I said to him, 'Do you know where you are?' and he said, 'Wedding day,' and he was crying.

His daughter had swum to shore, told two other guests what happened and they called for the ambulance.

At the shore the ambulance workers came onto the boat and took him to hospital. They were a bit surprised to see a bride resuscitating him. It turned out he had a heart blockage. He had a pacemaker put in that night.

We then drove back to a friend's house where I went to fix up my lipstick – and it hadn't budged. It was a Poppy lipstick. Ever since, I've been meaning to write to Poppy and tell her. I wiped it off and applied it again anyway after all that breathing on John's lips.

We finally got to the reception an hour and a half late but it was still a good day because he lived. I think a wedding's a blur for everybody. The only part that was ruined was the pre-drinks before the reception started.

When John collapsed I remember thinking, 'What the…? Do you mind, on my wedding day!' But it felt good to save someone's life.

When he came out of hospital they were playing 'Here Comes the Bride' on the radio, and he cried and said he was the first person to kiss the bride and that had made him happy.

John was incredibly thankful. His son came to see me the next morning and wrapped his arms around me and said, 'You're the best' and the love in his heart was amazing;

that alone made it all worthwhile. John later gave us the most beautiful cheval mirror that he had made for us.

The annoying thing was that my wedding dress survived everything, with me crawling around the bottom of the boat and so on, but then when we got out of the taxi at the end of the night it got grease on it. I later realised that the catering staff at the reception had taken my horseshoes – stolen all of them. But when I look back on my wedding day I still think it was a beautiful day.

How it feels to be a web cam girl

Livian, 23

When I was eighteen I moved to a new place and was pretty lonely. The Internet became my social life. I got pretty addicted to it and loved going to the cam-girl websites to read their diaries. I bought a web camera so I could take part in online chats and then I thought I might as well do my own site. I update my stills about once a day, but I don't do anything live. Sometimes it's pictures of me just sitting typing at the computer; other times I might put on a show.

The first time I got to 100 hits, it was like 'Wow' – then I wondered if I could get 200. At my peak I was getting about 3,000 hits a day.

A lot of girls want to make money from their sites by being amateur porn stars. For me it was more about having an online journal of my life. Yeah, I might be an extrovert, I might be into subtle nudity, but I'm not into porn.

You get a lot of offers from guys, and e-mails saying, 'Do you take naked pictures?'

Sometimes I have mucked around a bit on the cam – when the person you are talking to is on the other side of the world and you can't see them, it makes you do more than you really want to do; to show more than you meant to.

The first lot of cam girls coined the phrase 'cam whores' as a bit of a tongue-in-cheek thing. We were whoring ourselves for hits, getting on cam and flirting.

When I first got online I never thought I would do anything like that, but then here I was taking pictures of my cleavage and running around in my underwear. I really wish I hadn't done that now.

I guess when I was eighteen it was easier for people to get things out of me; it didn't take much for me to show a bit of flesh – they might compliment you, tell you how beautiful you are, that sort of thing. And then your hits start to increase as you show more. That's definitely something I played with in the beginning. Your hits skyrocket if you show a bit of cleavage. The trouble is you do it once and then the next time you have to top it and do something worse. Now I'm more jaded and hard.

In 2001 I took part in an online competition called SurvivorCam which had the tag line 'Outshine, outpose, outwhore'. It was just like the TV show *Survivor* where we had to do stuff and get voted on. I came second by doing a striptease.

I have a wish list on my site and a lot of people have bought me things in the past. I don't know what their motivation was. I make it clear that I'm not going to send naked pics as a thank you; I've never done that. Guys do ask, 'What do you want for naked pics?' But I just make it clear that's not my thing.

My site is linked to Camwhores.com which has a partner program – this means I get money every time someone subscribes to it after going through my website. I get about US$50 a fortnight these days. I also have a Pay-Pal button on the site so people can send me money if they want. Sometimes people will send $5 out of good faith. I have a wish list with Amazon.com as well, and people have sent me lots of stuff in the past – mainly books, CDs and DVDs, fairly inexpensive things. I don't get much any more. I'm past my heyday. I certainly don't have the hard-core fans that some girls have.

The weirdos out there do freak you out, but I guess I feel safe because they are usually on the other side of the world and it's not like they're going to come all the way to Australia to stalk me. They're just a text box on the screen – it would be more freaky if it was someone in real life coming up to you and saying those things.

I guess you feel like you're in a comfort zone because you're safe at home in your bedroom. In real life if someone asked you to take off your top, you'd say, 'No way', but when it's just a camera it's easier.

I often write about where I'm going and where I like to hang out, and I have been recognised on the street. I know there's a risk and I'm probably naive in believing that it's not a problem for me, but I don't really think about it much. Nothing bad has ever happened to me and I guess I'm a very trusting person. I live in this happy land of thinking it won't happen to me and I don't really concern myself with that sort of worry.

I just hope that someone among all those perverts visits my site because they are interested in reading what I have to say.

I always had a fantasy that in fifty years' time people would find my diary and read all about my life. Well, now people all over the world are reading about it every day and commenting on it – that's awesome.

I'm into that whole voyeurism thing. I'd love to run into people's houses and just look around. I guess that was one of my biggest motivations – to get people from everywhere in the world to see into my life.

How it feels to be a transgendered person

Sally, 38

I was born a male. By the time I was nine years old I had a very clear picture in my head of being a woman, being turned into a woman and living as a woman.

The first awareness came when I was six. I always knew that I was different, that I wasn't the standard macho bloke.

I didn't have a lot of masculine traits or male traits. I didn't know what to make of my thoughts. I honestly thought it was a vivid imagination, or some sort of fantasy.

When I was a child nobody noticed the turmoil I was going through, so I just put it aside and, as all transgender and gay and lesbian people find, you can't put such issues aside forever – they just keep leaping out of the subconscious into the conscious.

I grew up in Brighton, a nice conservative suburb of Melbourne, in the seventies and I don't think anyone knew much about transsexuals or transgender people.

I'd been cross-dressing since childhood. I started with my mother's clothes, but it was all really secret stuff. I felt guilty about it. I'd sit at home and watch TV or videos while I was cross-dressed and it was so calming – I felt like I was closer to my true self.

I made some vague efforts to do the macho thing as I got older, trying to have an interest in football and cricket and trying to play them, with very few successful attempts. I'd go out to parties with a crate of beer and talk footy but it just wasn't me and I think people could tell that I wasn't really being true to myself, even if they didn't know why. I was very isolated.

It was an exhausting inner battle from about nine to twenty-nine years old. I actually wrote an autobiography and I called those years 'the empty years'. I finished school, went to university, did accounting, got a job in accounting, had very few friends, very little social life and so on. I'd had a few relationships with women, but only one intimate one.

I didn't acknowledge anything until I was twenty-nine when I finally plucked up the courage to tell someone about these images in my head, and that was the proverbial floodgate opening. It just keeps nagging at you like a voice in your head saying, 'You're living the wrong gender, you're living the wrong gender,' and it just gets louder and faster until you deal with it.

I went to see a psychiatrist and I had about ten or twelve sessions but it wasn't very helpful because she was doing what I would call 'conversion therapy' on me, trying to 'fix' me.

I confided in a very close friend and she was really helpful and saw that I was sinking into a real mess. I virtually lost all psychological functioning. She helped me find a psychologist who had done her masters in sexual orientation and who explained that, regardless of the gender you are assigned at birth, you can have masculine and feminine characteristics and that's called 'transgender'. In my head something just went 'clang'. It was a massive relief. I remember waking up two days after the appointment, feeling this absolute calm that I hadn't felt for so long.

I bought a book on cross-dressing and realised it was pretty much me. I thought, 'Well, if I've gone this far down by denying this part of myself, I wonder what would happen if I accepted it and flowed with it.' Eventually the pain of living unhappily was greater than the pain of moving out of my comfort zone.

That self-acceptance was the key to it. I needed the knowledge to self-accept.

Having identified myself as a transgender person, I joined the support group, Seahorse Club of Victoria and started living as a cross-dresser, still working and socialising with old friends as a male, but socialising more as a female. There was a duality. Even though that brought some relief and there was less loneliness, it still wasn't enough. People began to notice that they'd meet Sally who was this outgoing, vibrant, confident person, but as my male self I was a shy, quiet introvert.

After about four years I couldn't live a lie any longer. While Sally could do anything, the male person was just not functioning – becoming more and more foreign to me. He, who wasn't really there in the first place, was being blown away.

I realised that I needed to live full-time as female. I reached the 'transition or die' point, so I made the transition.

I'm now living as a non-operative transgender. For some time I pondered having the gender reassignment operation. One counsellor put it very simply, saying, 'You have an operation to make yourself healthier and happier. Is surgery going to do that for you?' and I just thought, 'No.' A lot of my friends say they can't wait for their surgery. I didn't have that desperation; it wasn't for me.

I've been on female hormones for five and a half years. I've gone from flat-chested to a 38C bra, which was a pleasant surprise. The hormones have triggered a loss of hair growth, but there has also been a lessening of libido.

I've found a good place that does laser hair removal, and lost ninety-five per cent of my facial hair. I probably have to run a razor over my face once a week to keep any fluffy stuff down.

Sexually I identify as bisexual. I would probably be around eighty to ninety per cent attracted to women and identify as a lesbian, and ten per cent likely to be with a male.

Often I'm attracted to people who are bisexual because they can look beyond medical and social stereotypes of gender identity and see the person.

I hang around a lot in lesbian groups but I probably wouldn't have a relationship with them because they're attracted to their ideal woman and I'm not quite there.

There's still some distance for society to travel in terms of so-called non-operative transsexuals such as myself. It's almost like it's OK if you're going to do this weird thing, but go all the way; don't stop halfway, like I did. Sadly I think there is even an element of this in the transgender community; there's a hierarchy.

But I've decided: 'Well, this is who I am,' and I think it opens the way for good things to come into my life. Trying to live a lie takes up all your energy and now that I'm not fighting myself, but just being true to myself, I can get on with my life.

How it feels to die and come back

Ken Mullens, 56

I was in hospital following a heart attack. I was having lunch and I felt very strange. I had a cardiac arrest and then it was instant death, but I felt I was aware the whole time. It was a strange, strange feeling.

It was like when you wake from sleep, but it really wasn't sleep; then next thing I went into darkness – really, really black. There was just not one speck of light. I used to suffer from claustrophobia, but this darkness didn't concern me. It was peaceful, very, very peaceful, and then I felt movement as if I was going somewhere, but I didn't know where.

I was drifting, but I wasn't sitting up or standing up. I was just drifting in the form that I was in, whatever form it might have been. At what speed I don't really know but I know it was incredibly fast, as fast as electricity, you might say. That speed factor was an important point; it was very, very fast.

Eventually, after a period – I can't say how long because there was no sense of time – the darkness dispersed slowly, ever so slowly, and then a light appeared and it seemed as if it was a million miles away.

It was like a hundred thousand suns. Bright, incredibly bright. I could look directly into that light. It was so very powerful and ever so bright. Words can't really describe the magnitude of the all-consuming love experienced when in the light. And not only love but perfection, peace, serenity, calmness and beauty. I felt that I was safely home. I was overawed by the experience.

The wisps of cloud are the things I can still remember most clearly – I just put my arms out to feel those clouds and I couldn't feel anything; then I looked and I had no arms and then I looked down and I had no body. Strange as it must seem, I had 360-degree vision, because I looked behind me and saw I had no back. But I did fully comprehend the fact that I was probably the shape of a ball, but it didn't frighten me – it was a feeling of 'Oh well, so what'.

I felt that there was a form in the light that I could see, but it was only vague. I felt ever so humble. I felt that this was something greater than great and I shouldn't have been there.

I couldn't see much more than what I imagined would be a head, but there were arms or what I thought were arms in the light. They were outstretched and they raised me up. I felt ecstatic, but I still couldn't see into the form. I could look into the light, but I couldn't define that figure.

I knew what I had to do. I can't say words were spoken because there was no such thing as speaking – it was like mind language, and my mission was made very clear. I was to go back and help people overcome the fear of death. I would go back and write two and a half books. I've written two but I get apprehensive about the third!

The experience was just so powerful, so all-consuming that the difficulty I had as a free spirit was fitting back into the human physical form. I just didn't seem to fit – I'm not talking size; it just didn't seem right. I'd gone back home, back where I came from, and then I had to return here and fulfil this mission – help people by telling them that in death your mind, soul, spirit never cease.

Later I could tell people what had happened in the hospital room while I was dead. It was not like I was sitting on the ceiling, because I was travelling towards the light, but somehow I could also see what was happening there; I knew exactly what was being done where and when – it was like being omnipresent.

The doctor said I was dead for twenty minutes; they'd stopped working on me and started packing up, and then all of a sudden they said I gave a cough and I was back. Afterwards I went and spoke to all the nurses and doctors about it. They said that when I revived I was still black and purple. It was the longest time they'd had someone gone after a cardiac arrest before being revived.

I think I had to die to learn to live. It changed my whole outlook on life, my whole outlook on people. It changed me from a bigoted type of person to someone more broadminded who can let people accept what they want to accept. As a Christian I used to feel my faith was the only faith, but this experience made that view seem ludicrous.

I firmly believe that people fear death because of the uncertainty of how and when they will die, but I now know that death is just going into another chapter, another phase of your existence.

How it feels to win the Lottery

Roger, 53

I was a sergeant chef in the army in 1986. I came home one night and heard the draw on TV. My wife Kaye threw her biro in the air and called out, 'We've won it!' I had to check the ticket several times just to make sure.

We didn't have any money to celebrate that night so we borrowed money to buy a crate of beer. I rang my mother straight away to tell her.

There wasn't much sleep that weekend; we were very restless. We didn't know what to do or what to think. There could have been heaps of winners or we could have it all to ourselves. It was a long weekend so we had to wait from the Saturday night until Tuesday morning to find out what we had won.

In those days you didn't register or anything, so we had to hold the ticket in our house. It was hidden

59

down the bra; under the pillows – there were about ten different places.

We thought we might have won enough to buy a house – about fifty or sixty grand.

We were battlers – more than battlers at that stage. We were paying off a car, paying off furniture loans, like everybody else. I was in the army, hoping to stay there long enough to be able to buy our first house, and Kaye worked too.

Kaye always bought lottery tickets, she'd been doing it forever, but it was the first Quick Pick she'd ever bought. Some woman that Kaye knew pushed in front of her in the queue when she went to buy the ticket and Kaye just let her go – and that meant we got the winning ticket.

At two o'clock on the Tuesday I was in the car when I heard on the radio that there had been only one winner. I knew then that we had scooped the pool. We won $1.4 million. I was by myself in the car. I had to pull over and have a smoke, my hands were shaking that much. It's something that you don't react to, even now you just can't comprehend it.

We took the ticket to the bank and they controlled everything. We never actually saw any cash; all we saw was the bank account statement showing that the money had gone into our account.

I decided to get out of the army. I was only staying in to do my twenty years of service.

The first thing we did was pay off all the loans that we owed. We bought a house, and a new car each. We'd never owned a new car in our lives. We went to Singapore for a holiday which was a real big step for us – it was the greatest experience we'll ever have in our life. We'd never been overseas before; we could never afford anything like that.

I bought myself some nice fishing gear and Kaye refurnished the house. We had great pleasure in giving our other furniture to a friend who was really battling – she's still got it, I think.

But nothing was like we thought it would be when we won. You think it's going to be the best thing ever, but it's not. The best thing about winning was being able to give money to our family. That was fantastic. It was actually better than we thought it would be. We gave away $260,000 – $20,000 for each brother and sister and our parents.

When I gave one sister her share she started crying and said, 'You know what this means to me? This means I'll never have to work again.' That meant the world to me. She went and told her employers to shove their job. Little things like that meant the world to me.

Winning the money hasn't meant that Kaye and I have had no ups and downs, but I think it's probably brought us closer together. We're probably old fashioned, but we don't want anything in life except to have a decent little house and just be able to afford to do things. But that money doesn't last forever. Now we're comfortable but we're not what you'd call rich people.

The worst thing about winning was the way people treated us. In a small town like ours everybody knows you. Some people say that you change when you win money – but it's not you, it's the people around you. We got heaps of letters from people asking for money. People who I thought were our friends changed their attitude towards us. I got into a couple of terrific bloody fights in the pub so I stopped going. People would make smart-arse remarks about how I could shout the bar – just jealousy. In the end they drove us out of the town.

That's the thing that really pisses you off about it even now, the way that some people treat you – like you're different.

I know for a fact that I've never changed; it's never changed me any.

A couple of times since winning I've been walking up the street and I think: 'I've won 1.4 million dollars' and it doesn't mean a thing to me. All it means to me is that I don't have to go to work and answer to somebody. I haven't worked in a regular job since we won, but in the past fifteen years I've cut and sold wood every year to earn a small wage to pay bills and do what normal people do.

After twenty years of having the money, and a lot of bad investments thanks to people who were so keen to give us their 'expert' advice, things just went downhill. We lost $70,000 overnight when the stock market crashed.

Kaye was always very good with money. If I want any I just go and ask her for it. I'm a bugger for getting caught out down the street with no money. I never walked around with a couple of grand in my pocket. With our home and investments we wouldn't have a quarter of the money left now.

I'm into the simple things in life – a boat so I can go fishing when I want to, that's all.

But you know, life's struggle never ever stopped. The struggle is still there. Our son recently had a car accident with his two little girls – they were all fine, luckily. Our daughter is driving up and down the highway all the time and the worry about that never stops.

People think when you win money you're immune from all the shit, but you're not, you still cop it all. It's been a real battle with our two kids; they're like everybody else's kids. Money can't buy you health or safety. You worry about your kids all the time and now that they've got their own kids, you worry about them too.

How it feels to be crushed in an ice crevasse

Raina Plowright, 29

I was going to work on a penguin-monitoring program at Mawson Station in the Antarctic, but I was only there for three days before the accident.

We were being trained to use the quad bikes but the person leading the training accidentally took us through a crevasse field. The ice was very, very bumpy and very difficult to navigate so I was really concentrating. I saw a little patch of snow in front of me and thought I'd better be careful about how I got across it. I slowed down and suddenly my front wheels were just spinning on the ice and then my back wheels broke through the snow – it was a snow bridge over a crevasse – and I found myself plummeting down. My body was upright and the four-wheel bike was plummeting vertically with me. Even though I must have been falling for just a millisecond, I had enough time to think: 'I'm falling – this is it.'

I always thought when someone fell off a cliff it would happen so fast they wouldn't know anything before they were dead – which I thought was good because they wouldn't have that horrific, awful feeling of knowing they were dying. But it's not true; you have enough time to know what's happening and to know it's the end.

The crevasse was at least 100 feet deep. It was very dark. The ice was a neon blue colour.

After falling about six metres the next thing I felt was just this enormous weight of metal crushing me as the 700-pound bike fell on me and wedged me into the ice. It was crushing my thoracic area and my abdomen, so I couldn't breathe at all.

I thought, 'Well, this is definitely it now,' because I couldn't get a breath. I thought I was going to die within minutes. There is not a word to describe that feeling.

It was extraordinarily unexpected – to be riding along on the ice and then two seconds later I'm dying. Here I am halfway down this crevasse, not able to breathe, and I thought: 'What a stupid way to die.'

I totally focused on figuring out some way to breathe. My chest was crushed, my abdomen was crushed, I had no mechanism to move air into my lungs. I had done a lot of meditation in the past and I don't know if it saved my life or not, but I pulled all those skills together to try to breathe and I was able to move some air into my lungs through my throat. I'm not sure exactly how I did it.

The people above came to the edge of the crevasse and were yelling down. I couldn't communicate back, but one of them asked me to wiggle my fingers and I knew it was really important to show them that I was alive. So I did it, but I lost control and couldn't breathe again and had to regain focus.

Very soon after being crushed into the ice wall I felt my legs go numb. It was like I had two heavy logs hanging from my body and I also lost control of my bladder.

I'm a veterinarian, so I knew instantly that I might be a paraplegic. That wasn't scary for me at all though. At the time I just wanted to live and if I was a live paraplegic that was just fine.

When the search-and-rescue guy broke the ice above the crevasse and came down to me, the first thing he did was to check my pulse and I just thought that was such a waste of time. I was on the edge of life and death and here he was checking my pulse! I was thinking: 'Just get me out of here.'

He put a rope around my chest and then attached me to his harness. They put a winch on the quad bike and started to pull it up. But the movement crushed me even more into the ice wall; I was being compressed into it. They pulled it up faster and then I got a real breath and fell into the guy's arms. A white curtain of complete despair came over me and I lost consciousness.

As I was lifted over the edge of the crevasse I regained consciousness and I felt this overwhelming feeling of 'I'm OK, I'm going to live.'

I had been down there for an hour and a quarter but I can only remember about three minutes of it.

They took me on the back of a truck to the medical centre. My body temperature was about thirty-two degrees but it was fifteen minutes before I started to feel cold. I was shaking violently and felt extraordinarily icy to the core.

I heard the doctor say, 'Her blood pressure is sixty over zero,' and I thought that just couldn't be right.

I had overwhelming nausea and started vomiting blood.

I just felt so awful; the pain was extraordinary. The next day they decided to operate. I had a crushing injury to the abdomen, bleeding vessels, a haematoma in my abdomen which was crushing nerves in my spinal cord, and traumatic pancreatitis. Both my legs were paralysed but one started to come back straight away and the other recovered in a couple of months.

I had a second operation a week later and then they sent me home by ship. I was in a rehabilitation hospital for three weeks back in Australia. I don't think your body is ever the same after injuries such as those, but I'm largely recovered.

How it feels to be suicidal

Grace, 35

I always thought suicide was such a dramatic, theatrical act. A tortured soul flinging itself into eternity. Now I know better. I know that suicide is not dramatic, there's no excitement or morbid thrill. When you feel suicidal it's literally the last gasp of life, when you can no longer summon the energy or will to continue living. There's no chilling crescendo of music as old movies would suggest; it's all dull and dark and hopeless.

That's how it was for me – and how it may be again tomorrow – I don't know. I hope the feelings don't come back, but as I fight my way back up to the surface through the stifling layers of depression, I've come to realise that the urge to die is insidious, it is just there sometimes.

At my worst I stood, a thirty-something, happily married mother of young children, with a successful career – contemplating a handful of pills. They looked so pretty, so inviting. I knew if I swallowed them the pain would stop and that's all I cared about.

Looking over my husband's shoulder one day as he flicked through a hardware catalogue, I noticed the razor blades. They sparkled so attractively, looked so efficient and clean, and I wanted them, wanted to feel them open up my skin and let the sullied blood flow away and take me with it.

I'd talk about these suicidal thoughts with people I could trust and without fail they all said, 'You're so lucky, your husband is gorgeous, your children are gorgeous, you have so much to live for.' I know they meant well, but as if this could make a difference, as if I hadn't already tried all that positive thinking. That's the point – depression robs you of the capacity for positive thoughts.

My husband cut a tendon in his finger once and we took him to the local ER where the nurse asked him to try to bend it. He couldn't and almost fainted when he realised that he had no control over the finger, that his brain was sending commands, but the connections were gone.

That's how being suicidal feels to me. My brain logically knows all the positive stuff but somehow the message doesn't get through. If the connection was working properly I wouldn't be suicidal. If I'd said to my husband, 'If you just think positive your finger will be OK,' the hospital staff would have laughed at me, yet every week I'm encouraged to think positive, not give up, count my blessings and look on the bright side. I do,

I do, I do – but my illness is as real as his cut finger and with all the will in the world I can't make it better by putting on a happy face.

Sometimes I get so terrified because I feel that it's inevitable that I will die from this… this pain. That in the end I will have no control or choice anyway; my body will take the only option it has for ending the hurt.

I don't want to die, I have never wanted to die. As I see it there are two choices: to live with the pain or to stop the pain. I'd like it to stop – it's unbearable, never-ending agony.

But yet, although I have cut myself, have counted the pills to make sure I have enough, have thought about where on my chest a gun should point to ensure a direct hit in the heart, and have contemplated buying a hose for the car exhaust, I'm still here.

I'm working through the depression and the shocking childhood trauma that triggered it. I'm doing all the right stuff: seeing a psychiatrist, taking the prescribed medication and talking, talking, talking.

I'm trying so hard to be well.

I'm devoted to my family and want to be well for them, and for me. I'm working so hard and sometimes the hardest part is that the illness and the work are invisible. I see mums at school rally around a parent who has had surgery – with casseroles, visits and flowers – and I feel isolated and alone. My situation is life and death too, but you can't see the wound.

I chat and smile and try to appear normal when I can, so outwardly I can seem fine. They don't know that I go to bed for days at a time, that I have dreadful nightmares, can no longer seem to work though once I was a workaholic, have taken to watching daytime TV and often feel so terrified and overwhelmed I'm paralysed. They don't know that I sit in the small hours of the morning reminding myself of the damage I would do to my children if I took the easier option.

I hate myself most of the time; I feel empty, shattered inside and deeply, endlessly sad for the childhood I lost.

I don't know how my story will end. I'm smart enough to let good friends and family know how unwell I am, and I promise to call them whenever the weather in my head turns ugly again.

I want to reach out for help; I don't want to be alone in the swirling ocean of my mind, where the water is frigid, dark and bottomless, the sky thunderous and dark and I'm cast adrift, desperately treading water – with no land in sight.

I want to get better, I want to be the fun-loving, motivated, involved mum, sister, wife, daughter and friend that I used to be. I want to achieve at work again, cook muffins and have picnics in the sun with the kids.

I want to put all the pieces of my shattered soul back together again – it will be precarious because there are shards of broken glass inside me and they need to be handled with care for they are jagged and will wound.

I feel as if my soul is a mirror smashed by pain. These pieces jangle discordantly inside me and I have to move through life carefully so I don't get stabbed by the edges.

But if I can just get this broken mirror back together, maybe one day I'll look into it and see reflected, me – smiling.

How it feels to be shot in the head

Senior Constable Neil Saunderson, 35

I was on night shift in 1992; it was just a routine shift on a quiet night. I'd been in the police force for less than a year at that stage. About 1 a.m. myself and the bloke I was with were just driving along Beach Road and we saw two guys running down the road. One of them was holding what looked like a briefcase. We decided to see what they were up to, so we did a U-turn and shone our searchlight onto the front of the houses on Beach Road, but we couldn't see anyone.

Then we did the same on the beach and we still couldn't see anyone, so we did another U-turn and parked the car out the front of the houses.

I was in the passenger side and I jumped out and walked in one driveway and my partner walked in the next one. I shone my torch up the side of the house, which had a big fence.

I looked behind the fence and there was nothing there either. There was nothing up the side of the house. I walked a bit further into the front yard and shone my torch onto the other side of the house and there was this figure of a man with a gun. The next thing I remember is the muzzle flashing – getting shot.

I sort of put my arms up but it was too late, and all I saw was the flash. It felt like the biggest whack to the side of the head that I've ever felt and I wondered what had happened.

I came staggering out of the yard and my partner thought that I'd shot someone, not thinking that someone else would have a gun. He came flying around and saw me with blood streaming from my head and said, 'What's going on?'

I said, 'I think I've been shot.'

We didn't have portable radios on so we had to try to wake up the neighbours in the next house but there was no one there. My partner jumped the fence to the next house and I sat on the doorstep of the neighbours' house.

The bullet hit me just above my eye, and broke the bone around my eye socket. It just missed my eye. It went towards my temple between my skin and my scalp; a little fragment of bone came out at the back of my ear.

The guy had a sawn-off gun. Earlier that night he'd threatened someone else with it. He was like a powder keg and I just happened to be in the wrong place at the wrong time.

Being shot was really painful. I've been hit in the head before, playing football or whatever, and it was like that but ten times worse. At the time I thought it must have been just a slug gun or something because I was still walking around even though I'd been shot in the head. You see people getting shot in the head on television who die, but I was still walking around and talking – it was pretty weird.

As I was sitting there my head was really aching and I felt pretty woozy. The wound just kept bleeding and with all the blood I realised that it wasn't very good, it was pretty serious.

The person who lived in the house where I got shot came out and said the offender had pointed the gun at him as well and had then taken off up the street.

Finally an ambulance came and took me to hospital and they operated on me that morning and took the bullet out. I've still got it in a container. I only spent about five days in hospital but the pain was pretty bad for a while afterwards.

On the X-ray the situation looks worse. The doctors said I was lucky because the bullet only just missed my brain and, because it was so close to my eye, I could have lost my sight too. If the bullet had gone through the eye it could have caused massive damage.

As it was, because of the power of the weapon, or maybe because I have a thick head, the bullet didn't penetrate my skull.

People go, 'Gees, you're lucky,' and I say, 'Yeah, well I was, but still it was pretty unlucky to get shot in the first place.' But I suppose I do feel lucky that nothing serious came of it.

I'm six foot five and people joke that if I was shorter, it would have missed; it would have been just a warning shot over the head of a short bloke.

Afterwards, leaving the police force didn't really cross my mind. I'd only been a member for less than a year so I was fairly keen on the job. I thought of it as the classic scenario – just get back on the horse.

I was off work for about a month after the shooting and then did day shift and office work for a while. I got offered counselling but didn't take it up. I felt good in myself. The police force were great; they offered me everything and let me have my space. They didn't push me into anything afterwards. They wanted to be quite certain I was all right before I went back into any normal shifts.

A couple of weeks later they caught the guy who shot me. The other bloke who was with him had run off onto the beach that night; he'd just crapped himself and gone. Later he told someone about what had happened and word got around, and that's how they got the first bloke, luckily enough. He was charged and got nine and a half years. I know where he is now and what he's doing. He's a fairly violent bloke.

It was a strange sensation the first time I worked at night again. Walking into the backyard of a house in darkness on

a windy night was difficult – it wasn't a hairy situation but
it still felt strange.

How it feels to survive a plane crash

Melissa Holland, 31

There were six of us, all nurses, on board the plane. I was the youngest at just 25. We'd been to King Island for a short holiday and were taking off from the island airport to go home to Victoria.

As we took off we heard a 'beep, beep, beep' and I had no idea what that was. Lucy was the pilot. She swore, then she said loudly, 'Put your heads down.' I thought it was just a joke.

Janey, the copilot, who was studying to become a qualified pilot, turned around and said to us, 'I love you all a lot.' And I said, 'I love you too.'

I can't really remember much, but I can remember Lucy saying out loud, 'I love you…' and then the names of her children and husband.

Lucy said again, 'Put your head down.' I was looking out the window but the woman opposite me, Susy, repeated, 'Put your head down.'

When I realised it was serious, I looked around and the others had their heads down so I knew that something wasn't right. Reluctantly I put my head down too.

Then the only thing I could remember was that something hit my mouth hard and I lost my two front teeth.

I don't know if I dreamt this or not, but when the plane crashed I looked up and I remember Janey's arm was twisted behind her back, and then I must have passed out.

We crashed onto the airstrip and a guy from the airport – a fitter and turner – resuscitated me.

Lucy, Janey and Susy all died. Another friend who was with us – she was about sixty-five – went home that night with minimal injuries, but she felt very guilty, thinking that she should have died because she'd already had most of her life. Another friend who was in the crash, Katy, has had a few back operations since the crash.

I feel a bit guilty too. Susy put her head up to tell me to put my head down and I think I lost my two front teeth because our faces crashed. She had just got engaged.

Janey was in my heart – my closest friend, and sometimes I get really pissed off and I think, 'Why did my friends die?' and then I tell myself tomorrow will be a better day, and I hold onto that.

After the crash I was taken to the Alfred Hospital by helicopter with severe brain injury that left me in a coma for fourteen weeks and in hospital and rehabilitation for a year and a bit. I died a few times during the first weeks but I have no memory of it at all.

I only started to be aware of things when I was transferred to Bairnsdale Hospital. When I got there I was slowly becoming conscious of what was happening, but I had no idea why I was there. I had dreamt that we got home safely. I dreamt so much when I was in the coma. I dreamt I was nursing again and had passed the naturopathic course I had been studying.

I woke up properly when I went to the Caulfield Rehabilitation Centre. A neurological psychologist came and spoke to me. I had an alphabet board to communicate with and I spelled out: 'Why am I here?' and she told me I was in an accident. She said an airplane accident. She told me that three of my friends died. From then on I was determined to get myself moving – to start walking and talking again. The doctors told my friends I would end up in a nursing home as a vegetable, but my friends told my doctors no, that wouldn't happen.

It's been a good battle because I'm still here. I value everything now and truly realise that you only live once, and I appreciate the weather, the water, the beaches, people – everything.

Especially I value all the people who helped me so much to get through this; it was their support and friendship that enabled me to move forward. But I think I've come as far as I have because of my own determination and courage too. I want to become 100 per cent again. I don't want to be depressed and upset. Because of my head injury I'm supposed to be depressed, but I'm not.

Learning to walk again was hard, really hard. My physiotherapist would tell me what to do, but I would swear at her – I was never nice.

My right side is not good at all because of the head injury and I fractured my back as well. When you have a stroke it affects one side of your body and it's like I've had a stroke. I also shattered my elbow and left ankle and fractured my ribs.

Most days I have pain from my back, and my arm is uncomfortable all the time, but I'll soon be having my last operation when they'll fuse my elbow more. I don't know how many operations I have had altogether – probably about four on my arm.

I'm happy I'm here. I really believe that I'm here for a reason; I think God wants me to achieve my aims. My girlfriends who died are with me every day; I could cry just talking about it.

I really appreciate the people who are in my life now. I appreciate everything around me too, and the good news is I'm allowed to become a nursing aide after I've done a re-entry course. I'm so excited about that.

In my head I told myself that I was going to move forward, that I was going to nurse again, that I was going to meet a lovely man and get married. All my life I've had to handle things, and I know the reward is going to be fantastic when I succeed.

How it feels to survive bacterial meningococcal disease

Peter, 23

I'd been out with a batch of friends; they came back to my place and we had a few drinks. The next morning I woke up and felt bad, but thought it was just a hangover. I had a really bad headache and stiffness throughout my whole body. I felt quite nauseous and my eyes were really sensitive to light. Just walking down the hallway was a real problem.

I went downstairs and told my parents that I felt pretty ill and needed some painkillers. Nothing really helped so an hour later I went to the GP. By that stage I thought that it probably wasn't just a hangover, because I've had a few of them, but this was pain I really just couldn't take.

After looking at me the doctor said he thought it was just the flu and to go home, have a few more Panadol and sleep, which was really the worst thing I could have been told. But you know, you trust your doctor. So that's

83

what I did. I did mention the possibility of a virus or meningococcal but he said no.

Nine hours later it had gotten much, much worse – almost unbearable. Any little movement I made was really painful. I sat there without moving all day in incredible pain.

I had stiffness and the headache was like a migraine, but much worse than any migraine I've ever had. There was full body pain as well – pain everywhere.

I started to think about what else it might be, whether the doctor was wrong and what I should do. When my parents came home from work we decided it was time to go to hospital.

When I started moving and had to switch on the light then I really knew how intense the pain could be and how sensitive I was to the light.

Travelling in the car was quite a bad experience; every little bump we went over made me shout out in agony. I became quite aggressive towards my mum because I was in such pain.

Dad told the hospital staff that he thought I might have meningococcal so I was rushed into emergency.

As I'd been lying down in the dark all day I hadn't checked my body for any rash. The doctor lifted my shirt and I had the beginnings of a faint rash on my stomach, arms and legs. But it wasn't like you often see on the television, not that dark rash.

How it feels to survive bacterial meningococcal disease

By the time the rash comes out it can really be too late, so I was pretty lucky that I got to the hospital when I did. They took some blood and gave me antibiotics straight away.

My legs in particular were really painful. I couldn't manage the pain at all and the doctors told my parents that my legs might need to be amputated.

I was in a delirious state and, hearing that I had the rash, I thought, 'Well, this could be it for me.' I realised that I could be dying and I was pretty afraid.

I was sad that I hadn't even made it to my twenty-first birthday. I had all sorts of awful thoughts about my family and how they might not cope, particularly my parents, or how it would be without my legs if I got through it.

They had to give me a lumbar puncture, to drain the fluid from my brain. I had to be awake for that, crouched into a ball as they put a large needle into the base of my spine. That certainly wasn't pleasant. After that they gave me a general anaesthetic. The next few nights I had very colourful dreams. Dreaming and sleeping offered the only break from the pain.

There were three days of pretty serious monitoring so that my condition didn't get worse, then I turned the corner and started improving. The doctors were pretty sure that I would be fine. I still didn't know if I'd recover fully or whether I'd be able to use my legs once I got better – that was my main concern.

I was in hospital for about three weeks, then I went home and spent the first two weeks in my bedroom, then another two weeks really taking it easy. It was at least a month before I started to go out and see people.

I can't really blame the GP for not picking it up because meningococcal is so hard to diagnose. I wasn't happy but that's just what happened and I hope more people and doctors can become aware of the symptoms.

When I was in the hospital I remember thinking, 'Why is this happening to me?' but now I think, 'Wow, I was so lucky,' particularly after hearing about a lot of other people who have died, lost limbs or been disfigured. I'm just extremely lucky, especially as it was originally misdiagnosed, and I did lie around for those nine hours before going to hospital – and that can be too late.

Luckily, I've recovered perfectly now. I can use all my limbs and I've got no scars, though it did take a while to feel comfortable doing everything and I was a bit slow for a few months after that.

When I got sick I was about halfway through a landscape architecture degree and was working in a restaurant. The illness really made me think about life; about where I was and what I wanted to achieve. It was almost like, 'I can start again – everything begins now.'

I'm now working as a landscape architect and I'm part of the Western Australian meningococcal awareness campaign through the Amanda Young Foundation.

I'd never really grasped the fact that I might die, until that happened to me. Now I put a lot more focus on what I want to do; before, I didn't have much goal orientation. The experience gave me more of a drive for life, which is still with me. Life is so precious you really have to make the most of it.

How it feels to be lost at sea

Derryl Huf, 62

We went out fishing about 6.15 a.m. on New Year's Eve. We went to a fairly popular place, about twelve miles north of the heads at Port Macquarie. We dropped anchor and the current was violently strong.

I baited up my hooks but didn't even put the sinker down. I wound it in and said, 'This is hopeless.' We couldn't fish in that current, so we went to pull the anchor up, and bang! That was it – we were capsized.

I had tried to pull the anchor up by driving the boat forward but with the current so strong – it was about four and a half knots – I had no hope of making any progress. The sea was becoming rougher; it did change rather rapidly and unexpectedly. Water was coming over the windscreen and canopy, so we had battened down the hatches. Then the anchor rope washed underneath the boat and got tangled in the prop just as a huge wave came, and – end

of story: we were capsized. I'd say we had about one and a
half to two seconds to do something, if anything.

Our mate Wayne grabbed a life jacket but my wife and
I were just tipped straight in. We had plenty of life jackets
and flares in the boat but there was no time to grab them.
I could only hope that we would be able to hold on and
keep our strength for as long as necessary in the water.

There was enough rope floating around for us to put it
through the eye of the boat. We tied the rope onto that,
and my wife held on to it, standing on the bow rail. Wayne
stood on top of the hull as though he was waterskiing,
holding onto the ropes. I was sitting between the outboard
motor and the boat, in water up to my armpits. I got
washed off I guess about thirty or forty times. I had a rope
lassoed around each wrist so when I'd get washed off I
would clamber back on again. Then a wave would come
up about a foot over my head but so long as I knew when
to hold my breath I was coping relatively well.

My wife, standing on the bow rail, was being banged up
against the side of the boat, but she held on for the whole
26 hours. She was so strong. The water was cold, but
you sort of acclimatise to it. We all suffered hypothermia
though.

I think if it wasn't for communication between the
three of us during this time we would have lost heart. We
were all praying and talking about our children and sort of
making plans – you know, that our daughter would have
our house and so on. We thought about our friends and

the fact that we'd meet them again one day in heaven. You think of all these things; you think you might die out there.

My wife offered God a challenge at one stage. She said, 'Righto, mate, if you want us to do more work for you, you've gotta save us.'

One amazing story was that just before evening my wife and Wayne looked up to see a silhouette cloud in the shape of a dove. The dove is the Holy Spirit's sign of peace and was associated with Noah's ark in the Old Testament story. Then the cloud formation changed into the shape of a vessel – a boat. That was fascinating.

During the night about a dozen or so vessels came towards us, but then turned away towards land, searching for calmer currents, thank you very much. We would yell and scream to no avail; it was very frustrating. The time wasn't right, I guess.

At about 8.30 or 9 a.m. a ship virtually came around the corner and Wayne said we should all pray that the ship's captain would steer towards us. Then, instead of going towards the calmer current he came straight at us and passed within 300 feet.

Wayne had salvaged a red coat that floated out from under the boat – it was my dear Massey Ferguson coat, which had been caught on something and ripped in half – and Wayne was waving that vividly and relentlessly. Then, when we thought: 'Oh well, the ship's gone past,' suddenly it slowed and did a right-angle turn. We'd been sighted. And how fascinating – the ship's name was *An Angel*.

It was just in time for me. When I got washed off the boat the last time, I had just about run out of all my reserve power. I thought: 'Boy, oh boy, I can't take too much more of this.'

The ship immediately called the helicopter rescue service; three of them arrived about a quarter of an hour later. What an experience being winched from the sea! I'd seen it on telly, but now I've been there. I insisted my wife was the first one to be winched to safety.

The helicopter crew was absolutely amazing; they were so caring. When we got out of the helicopter, do you think we could walk? Not a hope in life. You lose your land legs when you've been out to sea for so long, and it's as though you've had about seven times too much to drink – nothing works. So I was taken to hospital on a stretcher.

Because I was pounded against the motor for all that time I had terrible cuts all over my bottom. My knee doesn't seem to work too well, but I think my sciatic nerve's been fixed somehow.

It was an experience that we will never forget and we praise God that we lived through it.

How it feels to go to jail

Debbie Kilroy

I was put in a youth prison when I was thirteen for truanting from school. I went there in my school uniform. It was quite horrific in the prison system at that time; we were all drugged and locked up and it was up to the psychiatrists whether they let us out or not. I was in and out of there until I was seventeen.

It's not as if I was a troubled teen – the only reason I became troubled was because of the abuse I suffered in the prison system. These days if kids wag school it's nothing, but I ended up in there, and because of how highly abusive it was some other young women and I escaped and ended up living on the streets.

When I was in there my father died and I was told by the matron that I'd killed him, and as a young girl I believed that, and so I then put myself into violent situations to be punished because I'd killed Dad.

Violence wasn't part of my life until I hit the prison system, but when you're treated with violence that's how you learn to express yourself. I ended up in other violent and criminal situations until eventually I was facing a mandatory life sentence in 1989 for drug trafficking. However, on the day I went to court, the police dropped the trafficking charge so I ended up getting six years and finished parole in 1995.

In 1990 in the prison, I got stabbed twice trying to stop a murder. I witnessed a close friend get stabbed to death and I suppose that's when it hit me that 'God, there's got to be something better than this in life.' I had children and I wanted to move forward. Then we had a forum in the prison and I was asked to speak about my childhood experience and I talked about my father dying. It was quite traumatic because I didn't realise that I had carried this message inside of me, subconsciously, that I'd killed my father. I knew finally then that it wasn't my fault and I could let go of all the violence in my life.

Once violence is introduced to you it can lead anywhere and that system introduced violence to me, and so I was violent and I was angry – very volatile.

When your self-esteem and confidence are so battered down you think you're no one and you can't do anything. That's why I started the group 'Sisters Inside' while I was still in jail, to support women in prison.

I got an Order of Australia Medal recently; I won the Telstra Businesswoman of the Year award in Queensland;

and I'm finishing my law degree. I've done a social work degree, which I started in prison – and now more women in prison are starting to do university degrees. I try to be a role model. People say 'Wow, if Debbie can do it, I can do it,' because I've been through the system like them. If we offer these women a way forward they will take it and run with it.

I've never come across anyone who has broken the law for no reason – just because they're bad. I go into a youth detention centre each week to provide support for young women, and at no time do I hear them glorify crime. I hear them talk about the horrific abuse situations that they're coming from and are going back to.

Most women in prison are there for drug-related crime and usually that's related to horrific childhood sexual abuse and physical violence. So you have these children growing up, enduring horrific physical trauma, and the only way they can deal with it, because they're living in poverty as well, is to self-medicate. And that's when you have to start using illegal drugs and that's when you collide with crime, basically. If we released all the women jailed for drug-related crime there'd be hardly anyone in there.

How it feels to be exorcised

Rachael Bornhauser, 57

In 1994 I was seeing a psychologist who suggested to me that I had multiple personality disorder, and within a short time I developed 100 personalities. I was very, very confused at the time, and lost sight of reality.

A neighbour suggested I see the pastor at her church. She and her family believed in evil spirits and I was desperate for someone to help me. I didn't know I was going to be exorcised.

I went along to her church. They took me into a large room where a group of people were sitting in a circle. I sat among them and they started to pray and chant – and I just fell to my knees and said, 'Jesus Christ'.

They brought some oils and started rubbing my body with it. They rubbed it on my feet, on my arms and hands, and on my forehead, and the pastor was leaning over me saying, 'Bring the blood of Jesus over this body,' and as she was saying it I started to make weird noises, just saying stupid things. Someone made a comment about letting the spirits go and so I started to scream out names. All the names of my personalities. They wanted to cleanse me of the evil spirits. I had to spit out the demons, they said. I had a whole lot of phlegm and I spat everywhere, calling out the names of these demons, and it was then I realised that I was crazy. The thought went through my head: 'I'm mad.'

But their chanting and praying was very affecting, it was really like a form of hypnotism. It was very scary; they can drive you to suicide. I would have done anything they told me to; if the pastor had told me to stab myself or someone else I would have done it. They had such a powerful hold over my mind. I really lost myself. They invaded my personal space shockingly, touching me all over. It was very disempowering. You lose your sanity. I lost mine completely.

They kept on rubbing me with the oil and then I started to sing very loudly and speak in tongues. It's like a gibberish, it just came out. I'd never done it before in my life. I sang at the top of my voice, singing to Jesus – and it was like newfound energy rose up inside me – and it seemed to go out of my head, out of my body.

I thought I'd found what I needed. The pastor called me her sister and said, 'You will work for Jesus now,' and said I would go overseas as a missionary. I think they were like a cult really.

I was literally spitting and vomiting for hour after hour.

I thought it would help, I thought I was crazy and that they were going to get these demons out of me and then I'd be free for the rest of my life.

I went there on the Friday afternoon and stayed for 30 hours. I had my two teenage daughters with me and during breaks in the exorcism they imprisoned us; we were locked in a room at the top of the church and had no means of escape.

I isolated myself emotionally from my two girls; they couldn't reach me.

It was unbelievable the state the girls were in. My eldest daughter tried to strangle herself with her own hands in front of me – she was hysterical the whole time. The church people were abusive to her at one stage, because she tried to go against them. They all started to grab at her. They ripped her stockings off her and ripped her clothes off her and were pushing her around and she was screaming and crying.

The girls were supposed to accept what was happening to their mother – to watch me lying on the floor being rubbed all over, with my eyes bulging out, spitting and vomiting, making a terrible noise.

They told my daughter her teddy bear was possessed and would have to be destroyed because he was evil. They told them not to look into his eyes or else the demons would get into them too. It's the sort of stuff you only see in movies, but it was happening to us.

I think it was one of the worst experiences I've ever had in my whole life. I think it was extremely dangerous. I still can't believe it happened.

In the end I was in the room with my girls and suddenly I just came out of it and I thought: 'This is mad,' and I said to the girls, 'We're going home.' I bashed on the door and said we wanted to go home. The pastor said it wasn't a good idea, but I insisted, and reluctantly they drove us home.

I didn't have any more contact with them, but I continued their work on my two girls; I started exorcising both of them. I thought I had to get rid of their evil spirits as well. I would rub them with oils and pray to Jesus Christ. But my husband saw what I was doing and tried to have me committed – it was really crazy behaviour. The exorcism ended my marriage; it made me crazier.

It wasn't until about 1999 that I began to see some reality. Now I know that I was psychotic and what happened in that church made me worse. I've worked so hard to clear my head and stay stable since then. I'm being treated with anti-psychotic drugs and I'm seeing a psychiatrist. I'm a different person now. I've abandoned the idea of evil spirits.

How it feels to be told you're dying

Joel Nathan, 63

It was 1983. I had been feeling terrible for months but the doctors couldn't work out what was wrong with me. My blood counts kept falling and it was like living on a tightrope. I was getting more and more tired by the day and kept thinking it was because of work pressure. At that stage I was creative director of an advertising agency. I felt that I was paddling against the tide all the time.

Eventually one day the doctor said, 'We've got a name for it – you have a rare form of leukaemia.'

My response was one of absolute disbelief. I asked, 'Is this malignant?' and he said, 'Yes.' I said, 'How long have I got?' – it all felt like something out of a movie script. He said, 'I don't know.' I asked what could be done and he said, 'Nothing.'

I was in a state, as most people are when they're told such dreadful news – an absolute tailspin. I walked out

99

of there and sat in my car for about an hour and thought: 'No, this isn't happening to me… but it is,' and then: 'Sod the doctor, I'm going to do something about this.'

That was the beginning of a fifteen-month odyssey of looking for every alternative treatment that you could imagine.

I tried everything. I went to spiritual healers, faith healers, I went on seven-day fasts, and I meditated until I was stressed out of my mind. I became a vegan. Everybody thought I had lost it completely because there I was making wheat grass juices and coffee enemas, drinking raw liver and carrot juice.

When I look back on it I realise that when people are diagnosed, even the most intelligent person suspends their common sense and goes off in pursuit of all these unbelievably bizarre attempts to hang on to life.

Everybody around you is saying, 'Hang in there, don't give up,' and it's so hard meeting those expectations, let alone dealing with how you feel. You think, 'I can't be a loser; I have to try everything.'

Reason gets suspended. You try all these things, as I did, but nothing made a single bit of difference. My blood counts kept falling, my spleen got bigger. I'd wake up in the middle of the night with my pillow soaked in blood from nose, gum, eye and ear bleeds.

What kept me going was my belief that I would somehow get out of it. I wasn't in denial. I knew that I had a fatal illness; that I was probably going to die, but I wasn't prepared to throw in the towel. I searched and searched for information; I read up everything to the point where I could arguably claim to know as much as any qualified doctor about leukaemia.

It was just as if the whole world collapsed. One of the worst things was that my ex-wife said we mustn't tell the children, and that became a great strain. I eventually did tell them and it was the best thing that could have happened. They became absolutely devoted to helping me and, not surprisingly, two of them are doctors today.

I went through two near-death experiences at this time, both of which convinced me there was a power greater than myself; that the issue of deciding my own fate was possibly a myth.

There were times when I contemplated suicide, because I felt it was preferable to what I was going through. But then I thought to myself: 'I don't have the right to do this.'

I really came to believe that there was a God – not in the conventional manner, but that God was love, and if I could tap into this somehow I knew I would make it – but that if I didn't, it didn't matter.

I began to pray and to read the Bible avidly and I believe my prayers were answered because I came across an article, quite serendipitously, about a drug that was not available in Australia being trialled in America. I went to my doctor and said, 'I want this drug' and he said, 'It will take years before it's approved and, sorry, but you just don't have the time.' My response was, 'I'm not leaving until you get it for me.'

A week later I joined the world trial for the drug. I became the first person in Australia to be treated with Interferon, which is now on the free list.

It was horrendous treatment but I got through it and it held me for a few years, but then it began affecting my heart so I began looking for another drug. I found another being trialled in the US and fought hard to get it. The drug, Leustatin was administered by a seven-day infusion and put me into remission for several years, but then I had a recurrence. I had another treatment and, touch wood, since then I've never had any sign of the leukaemia. That's pretty amazing.

After that it was as if every day was a bonus. I've looked at it as a whole new life. I never went back into advertising. I started counselling people with life-threatening illnesses and wrote two books: *Time of My Life* (Penguin) and *What to do when they say it's Cancer – a Survivor's Guide* (Allen & Unwin).

My health continued to be rocky. I have had lung cancer, had a five-way heart bypass and kidney failure, but right now I'm in good health.

Through all this I came to understand that we're all part of something, we're given a gift of life and the worst thing we can do is to destroy that gift by immersing it in fear. The greatest obstacle in life is the fear of death. Fear of leaving your loved ones behind, fear of not fulfilling your potential.

Death sits at the bottom of it all and no one talks about it. Unless you confront it and deal with it you can't live life to the full.

I think that death is a gift. If there was no such thing as death we'd never do anything, we'd never create anything, it's a very important part of life.

How it feels to drown

Sue Merrotsy, 41

I was surfing as normal one day; I got off the board in chest high water and went under the water. The other guys surfing with me thought I'd gone under to look at fish. When I didn't resurface after about four minutes one of them paddled over to me, by which time I'd been under a few more minutes. He pulled me out and dragged me to shore.

I was grey, not breathing, and my lungs were filled with sand, and there was no air in them. I was dead for about ten minutes. The guys did CPR, then a couple of doctors came to help. The paramedics arrived and used a defibrillator to shock my heart.

My throat had closed up so they had to put a steel thing in it, and an air tube to pump air in. They got my heart going after the third shock, then the helicopter arrived and they flew me to hospital.

When they started my heart on the beach, apparently I said two things: 'It wasn't my time to go yet,' and 'The videos are due back.'

I don't remember any of it; friends have since told me what happened. I lost two days. I don't remember going for a surf, I don't remember anything.

I was on life support for three days because my body had shut down. The doctors told my children that I had an 80 per cent chance of dying. My sister-in-law even sent for the priest to give me the last rites.

They said my brain was twice the normal size because all the water got in and swelled it; the doctors said I had an excellent chance of brain damage because of the lack of oxygen. I woke up three days later in the wards. When I first woke up it was very hazy but within a few days I was back to normal and had no lasting damage. The doctors have said my survival was a miracle and extremely rare – to be gone for ten minutes, come back and suffer no visible effects.

No one knows why I went under the water. People suspected I might have hit my head, but I had no abrasions. They did tests a month after the accident and said I had the heart of a twenty-year-old.

About four weeks after the accident I went for my first swim and I don't know if this is something I created, but when I went under the water I had a clear image of myself lying under the water; lying there dead with my eyes open, very aware and just feeling so happy. I can't explain it. I've never felt such happiness and peace. When I came out of the water again I started crying; I was really angry and upset. It was like: 'Oh, that was so nice.'

I can't explain how it happened. I do know that before the accident I was in a really abusive relationship. I'm talking really abusive; physically and mentally. I'd got out of that finally, after about two and a half years. After the accident my counsellor suggested that maybe, because the guy still kept harassing me, a part of me just lost faith, thinking I would never get away from him, and so that part of me just thought: 'Well then, fine – I'm going.'

I have to give some credence to that possibility, because I remember that I felt powerless and I didn't know what to do any more and I didn't know who to speak to. I didn't know how to stop this person. All the stress of going through that may have created a high amount of adrenaline in my system and that could have been the reason I just slipped underwater. It wasn't intentional, but when you have been through years and years of abuse you feel very powerless. I'm educated and intelligent, but when it comes to things like that it doesn't matter who you are, you can get caught up in a cycle you don't know how to get out of. There was also the chance that it was a heart virus which can just come and go, boom, like that.

I really think it was a big shake-up for me, not at the exact time of the accident but in the six months afterwards

– that's when I decided I want the best of everything; that's when I met my new partner; that's when I got accepted to study law; that's when I started a stained glass window business and I love doing that.

After the accident the local surf club raised $5,000 for my family. It made me feel really loved and part of a community. It was lovely – there was money left in envelopes at our door, the lawn was mowed and I didn't know who had done it – those sorts of things. The accident showed me how wonderful strangers can be, how wonderful friends and community can be, and, you know, if they could all support me, then what the hell was I doing not supporting myself?

It was three months before I went surfing again. A month after the accident they put a defibrillator in the muscle above my left breast, so if my heart stops or goes into arrhythmia this will restart it. It's a $70,000 precaution. It looks a bit like a third breast because it sticks out, but the deal I've made with the doctors is that if it stays there for five years and doesn't go off, then they'll take it out and I won't have to have it replaced. So far my heart has behaved perfectly every day.

These days I spend about four to five hours a day surfing.

I have my dogs, I go for walks, I study, I've got my stained glass business, I read and I listen to music, but surfing is my real passion.

How it feels to contract dengue fever

Emily, 38

I went for a three-week holiday to Thailand with a girlfriend in 1989. We flew into Bangkok and had to trek to get to our destination of Ko Samui, which was a really out-of-the-way place in those days.

We didn't have any accommodation booked; we just went on an adventure to see what would happen. We had had all the right immunisations and so on before we left.

The first night we were there, we stayed at the first bungalow that we could find. The next day we set out to find a better place. We got lost on this island where there was no transport. We met a Thai guy who invited us to stay at his place; he also lined us up with a French Naval Seal who had a Japanese sailing junk – a beautiful, beautiful boat. This man organised for us to go to a local island and travel around with him, and that's where I got dengue fever on an island called Ko Pha-Ngan.

It was a very big druggie island, but we didn't know that. When we came back from there I was covered in welts from mosquito bites; it was the only day I got bitten.

Seven days later we flew out and I was starting to feel a little unwell. I think if I'd got sick in Thailand I would have been as dead as a doornail pretty quickly. We got home at 7 a.m. and that night I was supposed to do a nursing shift but I had started violently shaking. I thought it was because I was cold after coming from such a hot climate. I went to my GP and she said I had the flu. I asked for a blood test, but she refused and sent me home.

That night my mum went out on her first date with the guy who is now her husband. I said, 'Go out, I'll be fine.' Two hours later I rang my dad because all my joints had started freezing up. It was like rheumatic freeze in the joints – I couldn't move.

They got me into hospital but the doctors had no idea what was wrong, and it was awful, awful. My eyes bulged out of my head and I couldn't stop shaking. For six days they didn't know what I had. I was so photophobic they had to nurse me in a black room.

I had an endless string of doctors and specialists coming in to see me and it was just awful because they also had all the medical students, everybody, in there. I had so many people around my bed poking and prodding, and so many blood tests.

I couldn't move because the headache was so severe. My cell count was pretty much nothing at that stage and every part of my body was frozen. My platelet count dropped and then I started to haemorrhage from every organ, every part of my body. If water touched my skin it was like boiling hot acid attacking me.

I lost almost all my hair – it just fell until I had about twenty per cent of it left. I lost a huge amount of weight and looked just disgusting. I was completely covered in a dreadful red rash and had the worst pain in my eyes you could ever imagine. It was horrendously, horribly painful but I was too sick to worry about whether I was dying or not.

I was also concealing another problem from the hospital staff, because they had all these young, really gorgeous doctors. As I was coming out of the fever and was able to open my eyes and look around, I saw all these stunning men coming into my room. I couldn't tell them that years ago I'd had a horse-riding accident, and now, because of the fever, a major haematoma was forming between my legs from that previous injury. I had like three massive sausages swelling in my girly bits. I sat on that for weeks in the hospital, just swelling and swelling. I was too humiliated to tell them, even though I was a nurse and I knew what was happening.

When I was finally discharged from hospital I got into the car with Mum and said, 'You've got to take me to the GP.'

The GP just looked at me and said, 'Holy shit, you need to be in hospital right now.' But even he grabbed all his associates and said, 'You've got to come in here and look at this, so you'll know what it is if you ever come across it.'

I was readmitted to a different hospital that night and was operated on by a gynaecologist and had everything reconstructed down there, which has left me permanently impaired. They had to drain it all and rebuild it. I've been left with changed anatomy.

After I left hospital the infectious diseases doctors called me and said what I'd had was haemorrhagic dengue fever. It was six months before I felt normal again. I missed a semester of university because of it.

They told me the fever would never come back, but it did come back. I spent a few years with it coming and going, when I'd start shaking again and feeling sick. But it seems to be over now.

How it feels to be attacked by a crocodile

Val Plumwood

I was in a canoe on a tributary of the East Alligator River in Kakadu, looking for Aboriginal rock paintings. I had been out the previous day and it had been idyllic. This day, though, there was drizzle which progressed into torrential rain.

In the afternoon I had a strong feeling of being watched and suddenly the canoe seemed very flimsy. I had a sense of danger or vulnerability and decided I wanted to get out of there.

I started paddling down the river and hadn't got very far when I saw what looked like a stick ahead of me. As I was swept towards it I saw eyes in it and realised it was a crocodile. From what I could see, I thought it was probably a small one, so at first I wasn't alarmed. I'd seen small ones on previous days. It turned out that I was wrong and it was probably about eight to ten feet long.

I was almost past it when there was this great blow on the side of the canoe. I started paddling furiously but it followed, bashing on the canoe. I started looking for a place to get out, but couldn't see one. I felt sheer terror. This wasn't something I'd never thought about – but I'd been led to believe that canoes were safe.

I saw a tree growing from the water near the bank and thought maybe I could leap into it. I stood up and got ready to jump and as I did so the crocodile came up close. I looked straight into its eyes and it looked straight into mine. It had beautiful golden-flecked eyes. I remember those very strongly. I did the thing you're advised to do, which was to wave my arms and shout and try to look fearsome.

Then I jumped, and it got me in mid-jump. I saw this blur, a flash of teeth and water as it grabbed me between the legs and took me down for a death roll. I thought: 'I'm not food, I'm a human being, I don't believe this.'

It seemed as though I'd entered some sort of parallel universe where I didn't matter – I didn't count for anything. Suddenly I was in a universe where I had no more meaning than a piece of meat. That's a hard thing to accept.

There was incredible, searing pain, but I was mostly concerned about the roll, which seemed to last forever; it pushes water into your lungs and you have a strong sense of suffocating. It felt like my arms and legs were coming off – a great sort of whirling sensation.

My head came up above the water and I coughed the water out of my lungs and started to howl with pain.

Then it pushed me into the second death roll. We came up again and this time right next to me was a big, solid branch, so I grabbed onto that. I hung on grimly, thinking I'd sooner let it tear me apart than go through another death roll.

Then suddenly I felt the pressure relax and I realised it had let go. I tried again to jump into the tree. This time it grabbed me around the leg. Its mouth was right around my leg and up around my hip.

It took me down for a third death roll. Again I thought I was going to die. I thought it was going to take a long time over it, which seemed worse than having it kill me straight out.

But a minute later it let go of me again. I tried to throw myself at the mud bank. I got almost to the top and then slid back down again. I did it again but didn't get as far. As I slid down the mud I managed to grab a tuft of grass and hang there. I found, by doing that, I could push my fingers into the mud and climb the bank.

I got up to the top and stood up and couldn't believe it; I was still alive. It was an incredible rush of elation. But because I was still in danger I floundered on. My leg wasn't working very well. I went on for some time before I stopped to look at my wounds. They were terrible, much worse than I had anticipated. The leg wound was particularly bad with bits of tendons and stuff hanging out.

I had shock right through my body and was feeling pretty sick. I tried lying down but felt worse so continued to walk back in the direction of the ranger's station. I felt just a glimmer of hope that I might survive.

The rain was still torrential and it took me a couple of hours to reach the lagoon I would have to cross to get back to the ranger's station. At this stage I started to black out and had to crawl. But then all of a sudden the rain stopped and the whole area became still, abnormally still, and so the ranger was able to hear me shouting for help.

It was then a thirteen-hour trip to Darwin Hospital, and I eventually recovered after almost a month in intensive care.

It was really a life-changing event for me. It was quite a while before I took in the full extent of how it changed my way of looking at the world. I have an incredible sense of feeling that life is not something to waste. I have a real glow and sense of gratitude about being alive, which has never left me.

The experience also changed my outlook. I had a sense that the experience was a dream, but I now think it's ordinary life that is the dream. We don't understand that we are ecological beings which are part of the food chain – we're still fighting that.

The experience also had a big impact on the direction of my work. Afterwards I started writing about how we see ourselves as outside nature. I'm writing about the power of nature and our illusions, how we need to see ourselves as being inside of nature.

Your final moments, those life-or-death experiences, have an incredible intensity – that's why they have the capacity to change life. You see things at that point which you wouldn't normally see; it strips away a lot of your illusions about your life.

How it feels to be abducted by aliens

Peter Khoury

My first conscious recognition of being abducted was in 1988. I had just moved back in with my parents and one night I went into my bedroom, switched on the TV and went to lie back on the bed, but my head hadn't even reached the pillow when I felt something grab me around my ankles.

I instantly felt pins and needles crawling up through my legs, up through my thighs, and right through my body to the top of my head. When it reached the top of my head it just felt like static electricity or like thousands of ants crawling through my scalp, and instantly I became paralysed.

I couldn't move. I tried to call out but I couldn't make a sound. I was thinking: 'Call out Sam's name!' – that's my brother. But I couldn't.

I started to think, 'Oh my God, I'm twenty-three years old and I'm paralysed – I'm going to be in a wheelchair for the rest of my life.' I wasn't thinking aliens or UFOs – nothing like that. I thought it was some sort of disease; I thought it was payback for a fairly wild lifestyle. That's when I started to get really frightened.

Then, all of a sudden, I look at the end of the bed and there's a creature there, a being. Horrific-looking at that. There were either two or three of them between the wall and my bed.

I realised one of them had grabbed me around the ankles. I thought, 'This is evil, this is the devil. I'm dead; they've taken my soul.'

On the left-hand side of the bed were two beings totally different from the others. The first lot were about three to four feet in height. Imagine a gorilla's head that was very dark, with wrinkly, shiny, leathery skin. They had very big, round heads and were wearing robes with hoods, which made their heads look even bigger.

The other two were seven or eight feet tall. One was a female but they looked almost identical. They were wearing some kind of jumpsuits, with what looked like doctors' white coats. Both of them had surgical masks around their necks.

They had oval-shaped heads that came to a point at the chin; their eyes were very, very big, cowlike and almond-shaped. Their noses were very small and long. I couldn't see any teeth or tongue – their mouths were just one little slit.

The one closest to me was leaning over me. As soon as I looked in his eyes it was like I fell into a void and it just overwhelmed me; it was like he knew everything about me. There was a connection, as if he was speaking to me through his eyes – it was telepathic. He was 'saying' to me, 'Calm down, we're not going to harm you, it'll be like the last time.' That made me think, 'What last time? What's going on here?'

He had in his hand what looked like a syringe, but more like a crystal wand – a little tube with a tiny light at the point of it. He pointed it to the top left side of my head and pushed it in. I didn't feel any pain, but I blacked out.

I woke up and sprang out of bed, and the paralysis was gone. I thought I'd been asleep for only about fifteen minutes, but when I looked at the time it was 2.30 a.m.

The only memory I had was of being in a round room where the walls emitted light. It was like being inside a pearl. I remember lying on a table and someone standing above my head and speaking like a bird chirping. It was one being, but it sounded like thousands of birds.

I was wondering, 'How can I understand what you're saying when you're talking at this speed?' and he said to me, 'You will remember,' but I can't.

After a shower the next morning I felt burning on my right shin; there was this red, raw mark as though a cigarette had been left to burn on it.

Six hours later I went to pick up my wife and I told her that something had happened. I went to show her the burn on my leg but it was healed. There was still a mark there, but it had healed after only six hours.

It's a deep, round scar about a quarter of an inch in diameter and it's got three marks on it, like a triangle, in the middle. It's called a scoop mark and is common among alien abductees. I've got about four or five now, but that was the first one I ever got. I also had a scar on my head like a doughnut; it was raised rather than indented.

I think what the beings are doing is treating humans the same way we treat animals facing extinction – catching them and implanting them with a tracking device. I think they need to track us. I have no doubt that a lot of people are being tracked – I have no doubt that I'm being tracked. My son also has an implant in his hand. You can see that there's something under there but we don't want to say much or do much about it. He's OK, my kids are OK with it, they're not scared or anything.

I've never been fazed by what's happened to me. It's had a big effect on my life but it's been a really positive one.

The next abduction was in 1992. You'd think it couldn't get stranger than the first time, but it did. This day I drove my wife to the station and on the way I must have vomited about eight to ten times. I had to pull over each time and was violently ill. I said to her, 'Where is this coming from?'

On the way home it was even worse. I came home and went straight to bed. All of a sudden it felt as if a cat jumped onto the bed – we didn't have pets at the time. I opened my eyes and, straddling me – sitting on top of me – was a naked female. Another female was sitting on the end of the bed.

The one sitting on me was a humanoid in that she had arms, legs and hair. She had human features – eyes and nose, mouth, everything, but the eyes were more than twice as big as human eyes, and her nose and face were longer, more stretched.

I was still fully dressed but they were both naked. One of them was completely blonde and the other one was Asian, very petite, with a bit of a belly – she was sitting on the corner of the bed with her legs folded under her.

I was stunned. I thought: 'What the hell? How did they get here, what are they doing in my room?' I thought someone had broken into the house and tied me up. It took me half a minute to realise that it wasn't a dream – this was really happening.

Next I sat bolt upright and, as I did that… this is very hard to explain, but I'll do my best… it felt like my soul sat up quicker than I did, and as my body tried to catch up with my soul I could see myself. There was a kind of transparent image of me. It was really weird.

Then the female cupped her hands around the back of my head and brought me to her breast and buried my face

121

in her breast. I'm claustrophobic at the best of times so this was awful.

I pushed away with both my hands against her body but she pulled me towards her again. The third time she buried my face in her breast so hard – she had super strength – that I couldn't breathe. I don't know why I did what I did next – I've never done it to any other woman; I don't think any woman would appreciate it – but I took a little bite of her flesh; I think I bit the nipple and a little bit of skin came off and went in my mouth and got stuck in my throat.

She pushed me back, looked at me, looked at the other one and I could tell they were communicating and she was saying to her, 'This is wrong, it didn't go as planned' sort of thing.

I got the impression that they had done this with me before.

It was definitely a sexual thing – I mean she was naked and straddling me.

Because I'd swallowed this thing I got the worst coughing fit you can imagine. It was like a chemical reaction in my throat. It was burning the hell out of my throat. I couldn't believe how bad it felt. I'm coughing and coughing, and I look up and they're gone – vanished.

I left my room, went into the kitchen and ate some bread, and tried to wash this thing in my throat down with water. It was stuck in my throat for three days. Afterwards I wished I had vomited it out or coughed it out. It might have been good DNA. People asked me later if I checked for it in my bowel motions, but that never crossed my mind.

Then I had the urge to wee, so I went to the toilet and, as I was about to go, it felt as if barbed wire or razors were ripping at my penis and… it's a bit private… I pushed my foreskin back and I saw two hairs curled like springs and stuck on my penis. It was really, really painful to remove them because they had dug in. It was like they were hooked in. One was six inches, the other about three inches. We don't actually know if they were from the head or the pubic area of the beings.

I think whoever was in my room were hybrids or clones.

I don't think they were fully human because when I bit on that nipple she didn't scream and she didn't bleed. Her skin was very, very pale, as though she hadn't seen the sun. Her hair was sort of blown back – a bit like Farrah Fawcett's when she was in *Charlie's Angels*.

At one stage one of the beings touched her stomach and I think she was pregnant. I believe they're trying to replenish their race because they can't actually reproduce, and whether it's because they don't have males, or their males just don't have any sperm, I don't know. I think they harvest sperm from us, and are building up their population or trying to produce a hybrid – someone who looks more human. I think they were using me for reproduction and that they had done the same thing to me before.

I kept the hairs and had them scientifically tested. The scientists tried to photograph them, but because they were transparent they had to spend about $10,000 to get a photo done with special microscopes. You can only just see them with the naked eye.

The scientists found that the hairs have a mosaic structure that our hair doesn't. They concluded definitely that it's not human hair – only two or three per cent of the creatures on this planet have a similar DNA structure.

It's been listed as the world's first biological evidence of an alien abduction case. So it makes the case pretty big.

The aliens will come back to me, without a doubt. All I wish for is the opportunity to ask some questions. I want to be a willing participant but at least I'd like a say in the matter.

I think their world is more dimensional than just simply being about space travel. I think it's right there, next to us, but it's in another density and they know how to manipulate it.

How it feels to have a breast enhancement

Lily Evans, 36

I hated my breasts. After breastfeeding four children they were like ski jumps – and basically all I had left were nipples. I had always been small, but now the shape was rotten too.

After I weaned my last child I went looking for a good-quality booster bra and couldn't find anything decent in 32A or 32B. The ones I did try just flapped around my nipples.

I was so disgusted I marched out of the changing rooms and decided there and then to have a boob job. I didn't have a doubt or second thought after that day.

My girlfriend knew someone who had had the surgery done and said it changed her life. She had done a lot of research before finding her surgeon and was thrilled with him, so I was happy to go on her referral.

I rang the surgery and made arrangements for a free consultation. I felt very intimidated at first but I was quickly made to feel at ease by the staff in the clinic who were just lovely.

I wanted to have saline implants but after they explained that saline sloshes around and can pucker I decided to go for silicone. I'm a very active person; the thought of my boobs sloshing when I ran wasn't at all appealing.

I met the surgeon at the next visit. I don't bare my boobs to anyone, but because he was so nice, I was able to relax while he drew lines all over my breasts.

I couldn't believe how quickly it could be done – it was basically three months from decision to incision.

I booked into hospital and on the day of the surgery nearly fainted with fear. I made my best friend kiss me goodbye in case I died under the general anaesthetic.

I woke in recovery with a massive headache that outweighed the pain in my breasts. I had a catheter in my boobs, feeding local anaesthetic into the area, and that really helped. I left hospital a few hours later and went back the next day to have the catheter topped up.

This was my first operation and the pain was much worse than I thought it would be. I've never felt that sort of raw, burning pain before. I took Panadeine Forte four-hourly for the next three days and really needed it. My whole breast area was painful. The pain really astonished me, and three weeks later it was still tender.

How it feels to have a breast enhancement

I had no bruising at all which really surprised me, and overall I'm absolutely thrilled. It cost almost $9,000 and not one bit is covered by Medicare, or private health insurance, but it was worth every cent. I'm now a 32C and very happy.

How it feels to be 'locked in'

Airlie Kirkham, 38

" **I was a** Japanese language teacher in Adelaide. I had a very satisfying and happy life. I loved teaching, enjoyed music and friendships. I had a wonderful boyfriend and friends from university where I had completed my arts and music degrees, and a graduate Diploma of Teaching.

When I was 25, I was driving along a country road to a kitchen tea party. I somehow found myself on an unknown dirt road. Going round a bend, I skidded into the path of another car (I was not speeding but my wheel may have caught the gravel on the edge).

I was in a coma for several weeks with a very severe brain injury and several broken bones, and I had my spleen removed. I was not expected to live. After the coma, I was very sleepy, but I remember my parents sitting by my bedside every day and night. I wasn't in pain.

128

Eventually I went to the Julia Farr Centre to begin rehabilitation. I was there for over six years. I recall big wards, many people who rushed around looking too busy to be friendly. The rooms were full of people like me, accident victims who were unable to do more than pass the time.

My time seemed to drag. There was little to do except watch TV and I couldn't see that properly. They put us to bed so early. How could we complain? Few of us could talk.

At times people would come and talk over me, not to me. Many thought I was vegetative, because I could not communicate or respond, or even move a muscle. I could move my right leg a bit but that was all.

I felt locked in because I couldn't speak or even write.

The 'locked-in' state is a diagnosis applied to people who demonstrate alertness and wakefulness but who cannot respond. I could see everything and everyone. I knew who they were. I could hear people talking about me and saying things I didn't like.

Since I could hear and understand, I would have liked people to talk to me properly. I felt very frustrated, at times angry, because often no one would come near me nor talk to me – only Mum and Dad, my visitors or therapists. I was frustrated because I couldn't make decisions, or tell people what I wanted. I wasn't in control of myself. I learnt to wriggle my finger, hoping someone would notice and talk to me. I wanted to tell everyone, 'I'm still here. Inside me is Airlie. I have so much to say.'

The seasons came and went. I made some progress but I was unable to assert myself or respond. I was bound by ritual, routine, habit, culture.

I set my sights on being able to communicate. Couldn't I do that? I had been an articulate person once. I could be that again.

After about five years my right arm recovered some movement. Then a miracle occurred. At Mum's request, the occupational therapist was asked to try and help me write again. She made me a special penholder and glove. The first word I wrote was 'Airlie'. Then I answered a question from the therapist who asked if I wanted to learn to write again.

I wrote, 'Yes. I need your help.'

At first I wrote like a kindergarten child. It took me over six months to learn writing again and I have not stopped since. The pen and its holder are my lifeline to the world.

I proved I was not vegetative but locked in. Now I was free at last. I felt I had the whole world opening up in front of me. I wrote down all my questions. I had so much catching up to do. I felt wonderful now that I could talk to Mum and tell her all my problems and feelings. It was like a door opening, and all my thoughts came pouring out. I felt so excited and happy now that I could tell everyone that my brain could still think, that I wasn't stupid or unable to understand. Even today, people often say to Mum, 'Can she understand what I'm saying?'

I felt so much love in my heart for God, who had answered my prayers for survival and had helped me communicate again, and for my family who had looked after me so well.

I turned to writing poetry. Poetry has always inspired me.

To other families with relatives in a similar situation, I would say, never give up hope; be strong and determined. You need to communicate to your loved one because even people in a coma can hear and think. They are sensitive to their environment and need to be aware of their family's strong hope and faith.

In 2002 I enrolled in a refresher subject of Bachelor of Music, and with the support of my carer and mother, achieved a distinction.

In 2003 I enrolled part-time for Bachelor of Music, Honours Musicology, and achieved good results. I still need total support for daily activities. I still cannot walk or talk, but I can think and communicate, using my pen and a delta talker machine which speaks for me. University is the best thing in my life at present. What the future holds I don't know.

The path of life that I tread now is not the path I would have chosen for myself. But I will walk it, with the strength of God whose steadfast love has never failed me.

How it feels to speak to dead people

Amanda de Warren

I don't do Tarot cards or use a crystal ball. I don't do fortune telling, I do channelling which is completely different.

I communicate telepathically with people who have passed to the afterlife.

Before I was aware of my skill I would go to the occasional psychic reader and have my cards read and I'd think, 'Oh yeah, whatever,' but when Eric, my partner, passed over in 2001, things changed.

Before he passed over we were always pretty much telepathically connected. I knew from the minute I met him there was something really special about him.

He died of stomach cancer. It started in his lungs and went down to his stomach and his bowel and just ravaged his whole body. It was horrific. But the minute he passed over I felt a warm, loving feeling and I knew it was still him. I was sitting there looking at his body and I heard his voice in my head: 'I'm OK and you're going to be OK too.'

The channelling took off from there. I had little awareness of this gift before he died. I'd never thought about the afterlife until then – never really given it a thought. But from the first day that he passed over, when I was thirty-nine, I was just thrown in the deep end.

I started hearing all these people and thought I was going crazy. There was a lot of chatter, people chattering in my head. I had to learn how to shut them off. I was scared but I decided to just go with the flow. I had a gut feeling that there was meaning to the chatter – that I wasn't crazy. There were a lot of supernatural things going on around me. I'd hear people running down the hallway and voices whispering in my ear. I'd walk into my bedroom and the drawers would be open.

I could feel a difference within me, like a strong sense of paranormal things, but I still needed answers. I was guided to quite a few people in the spiritual industry. I went to Richard Kid, who's been a reader and a very psychic man for thirty-five years. I went to one of his workshops and as soon as I walked in they all stopped and their mouths just dropped. Richard said, 'You have this amazing white light around you, I haven't seen this in years.'

He told me I had some very special quality and that he wanted to help me develop it. It was a strange time – I was trying to deal with Eric's death and then I was trying to deal with this as well.

In the beginning I had to learn to turn it on and off. There's good and bad on either side and I have gatekeepers to protect me. Once I open myself up, then the people come through. They show me who they are, what they died of, what their lifespan was, what their relationships were. I can have anything up to twelve or thirteen people come through at the one time.

Every so often spirits do pop in unexpectedly. I was having lunch a while ago; this was before I had really learnt how to close myself off properly, and I didn't know the lady who was sitting across from me, but I said, 'I've got your daughter here; she hanged herself in the bathroom.' This person told me a lot of detailed stuff that even the family didn't know.

I receive everything telepathically; it's a succession of pictures, themes, feelings – all sorts of things. I hear, smell, feel and taste – I get all of the senses.

You have no idea the number of people to whom I have given closure and peace of mind. I absolutely see this as a gift; it has nothing to do with notoriety, status symbol or celebrity – I just want to get out there and help as many people as I can to communicate with loved ones who have crossed over, just to give them peace of mind.

All the channellings I do are unique. Some are full of laughing and jokes, some are full of sadness.

I did a channelling recently and the subject's friend was waiting downstairs because she wasn't sure whether to join us or not.

I said, 'Has your friend just lost her son?'

And she replied, 'Oh my God, yes.'

I said, 'Your friend's son is coming through; he's only recently passed over. He was about forty-one years old and he was on a red motorbike; he hit a cow and broke his neck.'

She said, 'Oh my God, yes.'

I went downstairs and said to the woman, 'Your son's here.'

That's the sort of stuff I get coming through.

To anyone who doesn't believe this I would say, speak to my 1,500 clients, I do not have time to go finding out what my clients did thirty or forty years ago that not even their children know. Ninety-eight per cent of my clients will tell you the same thing: 'There is no way she could have known half that information that came through.'

I'm not sure why I was given this gift; I feel maybe I was fine-tuned for this, as though I'd been learning this over centuries. It comes naturally and I feel I am a chosen one. I'm a very, very strong woman and I'm happy to go out there into the world and say, 'Hey, I can communicate with dead people and if you don't believe me I really don't care, but just because you don't believe in something, it doesn't mean it doesn't exist.'

I do this six or seven hours a day and I say to these doubters: 'Can you give me one hundred per cent proof that there's no life after death? Because I'll throw my hat into the ring if there isn't. And you tell me where I'm getting this information from if there's nothing after life.'

I have a lot of inside information, if you understand what I mean. I've been put out there for a reason and my gift just gets stronger and stronger all the time.

How it feels to be sexually abused by a nun

Sandy Caut, 45

She was like a member of our family. I had gone to her for counselling when my husband and I were having problems in our marriage. She was a nun with the local church.

I think she planned it from the start. She chose someone who was vulnerable and had low self-esteem. She spent time grooming me and edging her way into the family, making us like and depend on her.

At first she would come to the house and listen to my problems, but over time, sadly, she entrenched herself as one of the family. She would visit randomly until it was almost every night.

She told me I was a bad mother, a bad wife, that I couldn't cook or clean properly. I didn't remember it at

137

the time, but I had been sexually abused as a child and I was in a dissociative state where I had just shut off from everything. I was living in a kind of daze.

Eventually she told me that I didn't know how to love my husband and that she would show me how. She said that this was one of the problems in the marriage. She kissed me on the mouth, using her tongue to teach me how to kiss. I thought I was stupid and that she would help me.

Eventually it escalated and she would touch my breasts and then masturbate herself to orgasm. Afterwards she would withdraw from me totally and sometimes she would say things like 'I'm very naughty today.'

I was quite sick at the time and she would tuck me into bed and try to touch me vaginally, but something repelled me and I wouldn't let her. She would become very angry and annoyed about that. Sometimes she was physically abusive, hitting me if she felt like it.

She also invited me on retreats with her and would come into my room at nights and touch me and masturbate herself. For me it was like not being there; I just withdrew from it.

I never felt any pleasure at all.

The abuse escalated over time until it was almost every day. I was in la la land – I just couldn't cope with what was happening, until we went on a family camping trip. She came with us and was in charge as usual. She set up the tent and made sure I was sleeping next to her, with my children on the other side. During the night she continually touched my breasts and tried to touch my vagina but I pushed her away and finally got up after several hours and went outside. I think I must have broken through the detachment – it was as though something shifted inside me and I realised what had been happening.

The next day I confronted her for the first time, but she said it was just a bad dream. That was where it ended. Almost from that time our contact with her ended.

I sought counselling not long after this and initially I had terrible guilt, I couldn't believe that I had let this happen to me. I learned that this is a very common emotion among sexual abuse sufferers; the feeling that you should have been able to stop it. I now know that she was an extremely powerful person. Her personality was very controlling. She edged her way into our life and took that life from us. Hers was very much a classic sex-abuser profile; they ingratiate themselves into your life and you're caught in a double bind – you think they are such a nice person and that you need them, and then their behaviour changes.

Ten years after the abuse happened I reported it, and soon after, she died. I have now trained as a counsellor myself and specialise in sexual abuse victims. I'm still angry that she never apologised for what happened but I have moved on and have made a better life for myself and my family.

How it feels to be an identical triplet

Martin McKenna, 42

We were born in Limerick, Ireland, in 1962, not very long after the Second World War. The people of Limerick were shocked when suddenly this six-foot blonde bombshell appeared in their town and had these blond triplet boys, each with one green eye and one blue eye. Being Irish, the townsfolk put two and five together and came up with the idea that we were part of the Master Race, Hitler's plan for genetic purity.

People used to ostracise us. They had a deep-seated hatred of Germany. They would paint swastikas on our wall and refer to us as 'the Nazis'. It was very sad, and it was very hard for my mother who had been a refugee. Irish people can be afraid of anything different, and yet three is the luckiest number in the Celtic mythology. We could have been seen as an omen of good fortune, but they saw it the other way.

Genetically identical triplets are very rare. There were three of us in one sack inside my mother, each fighting for our share of everything. I was the smallest, weighing two pounds one ounce.

My mother didn't even know she was having triplets because they didn't have all that fancy equipment in those days. So two boys were born and they put her back on the ward. Then she started complaining about pains in the stomach so they pulled another one out and that was me.

We had no immune system so we weren't handled by humans; they put us into these incubators. We didn't get touched until we were about five months old, so when we got home we wouldn't let our mother hold us – we would scream and struggle. We would cuddle together – the three of us, or if the dog came in we would cuddle with him. My mother always said that when we came home from hospital she was going to give us back; she thought there was something wrong with us.

When we were born it was a big hurrah – all the newspapers came around. A baby food company sponsored us, but we were allergic to the food.

I don't know the medical statistics of genetic triplets, but I do know that when I was a kid, there weren't any other triplets around. We used to walk around and we used to say to each other, 'There's nobody else like us, is there? We might as well come from Mars, hey?'

Our neighbours on the right side had twins, and on the left side they had two sets of twins. There was a fairy mound, a very powerful one too, behind the house. Maybe the fairies had something to do with all the multiples.

When we got older we would never go out in public because of the people pointing at us all the time. We spent a lot of time in the house and no one would take us out because we'd freak out.

Even our first day of school was bad. My mother took us to school the first day and we barricaded ourselves in the school; we wouldn't let anyone near us. The teacher said, 'There's something wrong with these kids.'

When we get baptised at the age of seven, well, we don't know what a priest is! We're in the church and there's all these horrible pictures in there. We thought, 'Jesus Christ, what is this about?' And there's this big font full of water and a guy comes out in a cloak, so we were very wary. Then he picked up John and put his head near the water. Well, we thought he was going to drown him, so we went up and knocked the font over, knocked the priest over and ran out.

We didn't talk for a few years because we had our own private language going; we didn't need to let anyone else into our little club. I can still talk it today and even now, when we get together, we use it. We laugh and we're just like kids again.

When we were growing up, if any one of us had to get flogged we all got flogged; if anyone was getting a reward we all got a reward. My mother called us 'johnmartinandrew'.

When I was about nine or ten I was a really bad little fella and I was pretty anti-Christian after that episode in the church. My school tried to break me. But I always knew when I was in trouble I could go to our dogs, two German shepherds that my mother loved. One day I got in some serious trouble at school so I ran home to the dogs, but the principal followed and I set the dogs on him. The next day the dogs had to be destroyed for being vicious, and I knew that was it for me with my mother; she wouldn't look at me after that.

I ran away and lived in a little cowshed. There were lots of kids living on the streets. It was a pretty dangerous place so I ganged up with a group of old dogs because I was pretty good with dogs. I wouldn't trust people because they all let you down, but I had my pack of dogs. I used to sit down and watch what they did, and I could understand their communication. There were no fancy words – the rules were dead simple. I thought, 'That'll suit me, to live like that,' and I stayed for three or four years. My brothers would come down and bring me food.

Me and my brothers would fight with the other street kids for a place on the back of the rubbish truck as it headed for the dump; we'd get our fruit and stuff from there.

Being a triplet has been a blessing though it makes you think of someone outside of yourself. I've been thinking about and communicating with another two people since before I was born. At fifteen I broke loose from the circle.

We were apart for about five years before I realised that I was just me, I had to stop saying 'us' or 'we'.

When we were in Ireland everyone used to point the finger at us and say we were freaks, but after we left and met up together in Australia or the US, people would marvel at us; they wouldn't call us freaks. We're tall – over six foot three and around 14 stone – so we make a striking picture.

I came to Australia with fifty bucks and I've had a great life. For five years I've been doing radio shows for the ABC as The Dogman, a dog behaviourist. I've published a book even though I can't read or write, and I'm about to start a documentary. I've got a beautiful wife and beautiful children and I don't think I would have achieved all this anywhere else.

John now lives in South Africa and Andy went back to Ireland. Splitting apart was hard. We used to say, 'What can we do? How can we break the magic circle? Are we going to be old men, three of us living in a house together?'

But even now, if one of my brothers is seriously ill I know it. One night I have a nightmare that a glass has gone through my shoulder; I wake up with a pain in my shoulder. So I ring Andrew to see if he is all right and he says, 'Yeah, did you have the dream too?' So we ring John and he's not there. Then his girlfriend comes home and rings us and says John's in the hospital after he got a great big piece of glass from a window through his shoulder. That sort of communication comes from being in the same sack together, the same crib together, from being in the same situation together.

We're 42 now and pretty soon one of us is going down – that's the logical order of things. We discuss it now and say, 'I wonder which one of us will die first?' and try to make a joke of it, but it's not so much the first one who dies, it's the last the one left alive, who has to write the last sentence and close the door.

I miss my brothers. If Andy or John was in prison I'd break them out, there's no question about it. I used to say nothing could come between me and my brothers, but then my children came along and that kind of changes the equation. Me and my wife went through hell with this. When Andrew and John came to visit she would say, 'You think more of your brothers than you do of me,' and I had to work all that out. It's like: Well, we're big boys now; it's time we started letting go of each other emotionally.

How it feels to be kidnapped and tortured

Maria Pilar

In 1973 there was a military coup in my country – Chile.

It was like a nightmare. One day you have democracy and the next day you wake up in a vicious dictatorship. It felt like a different country.

We lived under absolute dictatorship. They controlled all media so nobody knew what was going on in the country – there are no official records for 1973 to 1990.

I was still in high school and just seventeen when they first attempted to have me arrested for being a student representative. I heard through the bush telegraph that they were looking for me so I went into hiding and eventually they stopped looking.

I was the leader of the student movement. I felt very close to poor people and as a middle-class person I felt

146

very privileged. My heart felt connections with the poorer people because they felt true and real.

I remember being fifteen years old and I saw very clearly that my path was going to be for peace and justice and ever since I have walked that path and been in a position of leadership one way or another.

There was a master plan before the coup to go through the country like a tank and flatten everything that could possible be a threat – even seventeen-year-old high school students – just to signify the government's power. They would do anything that could be seen as a lesson. There was such brutality and viciousness towards the people. Chilean people are very peaceful people; we were the most economically successful country in South America and were known as the British of South America because we very closely followed the British model, when it was good. We had free medical care, free immunisation, that sort of thing, and the coup was designed to destabilise all that – none of that exists now.

The second time I was arrested was the following year, 1974. I was completing my first year at university, studying engineering. I was contacted by old friends from the Left, which was illegal – everything was illegal by then. I heard that there was a strong resistance movement going on underground and people were doing their best to stop the human rights violations – to help political prisoners, to stop the tortures and disappearances. I was writing articles saying that the spirit was alive and we would return one day to democracy.

I was arrested for that. They kept me in solitary confinement and deprivation for three days. The thing that shocked me was that a twelve-year-old girl was arrested at the same time.

They torture people and get them to give up names and find out what is happening. I was terrified psychologically; they threatened to bring in my family, my brothers, my mother. I was kept in a cell with no windows. For interrogation you were taken out blindfolded with your hands tied. You were bashed up a little bit and terrorised. For three days they put lamps on you like a spotlight. Your family doesn't know where you are... you just disappear.

After they finished with me they dropped me in a street late at night without warm clothes or money to make my way home. I think my spirit got a bit broken, and if not, my heart was.

I gave up the resistance after that. I was terrified. They did a really good job of terrifying me. I was so demoralised by the experience, particularly seeing that twelve-year-old girl – that really got to me. How can you deal with that? I don't know what happened to her; for all I know she could be dead.

I decided to leave the country for a while, so I went across the Andes to Argentina. I met my first husband in Argentina. He was a freedom fighter there. We went back to Chile together and got married in 1975 and tried to make a living. I went to work as a teacher.

In 1976 our friends were so desperate about what was going on in the country we just couldn't sit passively, so we decided to join the resistance with two of my best friends. We'd try to campaign for the disappeared ones, trying to release political prisoners and try to get the government to have some respect for human rights. Almost every household was touched; some member of the family was tortured or arrested or disappeared or killed.

I saw my neighbour's house being ransacked and the whole family being arrested – that was just an everyday thing. They operated with the same techniques as the Nazis. The years between 1973 and 1978 were the most vicious years of the dictatorship, when they killed and tortured indiscriminately.

Eventually the police got to me again and took me to their underground quarters where they had torture chambers.

I was stripped naked, blindfolded and tied to a metal bed. About eight men surrounded me. I was 21 years old, so they were being offensive and insulting and having a good time with this terrified young girl. They applied electricity to my genitals and breasts; I don't know how they did it, I couldn't see, but I know it's a torture implement they used.

The pain was horrible. It's a form of rape to have those instruments introduced into your vagina and on your breasts, to be naked, tied up, blindfolded and gagged while all these men are around you having a jolly good time.

It lasted until they felt satisfied with the results – you lose track of time – it was more than an hour though. They were all saying, 'We'll bring your momma and do the same to her if you don't talk' – anything to make you break down.

For me it was instinct for survival that saved me. It's well known that you leave your body in those sorts of moments. Your body is there and your mind is somewhere else, detached.

In another session I had to watch my friend being tortured the same way. Babies were also tortured. I know this for a fact because my best friend had an eight-month-old baby and they and the father were arrested and he was tortured. If he didn't break down, then they started on the wife or the baby.

Babies were killed in their mothers' stomachs. If the military had any suspicions of anybody doing anything to threaten the powers that be, they'd take the children, to get to the parents. Anything to break down people and terrify them. It was a reign of terror and they did it very well.

Later the Secret Police came for us. They put sticky tape over our eyes, sacks over our heads, tied our legs and arms behind us and threw us in the back of a truck. I thought they were going to shoot us or throw us in the water. I thought that was it.

After hours of a bumpy ride we arrived at a place I later found out was a concentration camp, and I was admitted by some military men who asked what the charge was – I was charged with being a subversive delinquent, that was my crime.

I was terrified about what the Secret Police might do. I was put into solitary confinement before I was taken to be interrogated. They give you a medical check-up first to see how far they can take you in torture, how much you can endure.

I was in solitary for a month, waiting for my turn to be interrogated. I could hear the tortures going on – there was screaming day and night. I never saw anybody, I could hear them though. Sometimes it was a child asking for their mother or begging for forgiveness.

When I arrived there was something bubbling – they had wells with acid, another way they used to disappear people. They also put people in cages and had people hanging from their feet. For me that was more about psychological pressure, worrying about what the 'Gestapo of Chile' would do to me. There were vicious police dogs everywhere, used to attack people, and now every time I see a dog I have to cross the street.

It was a month of waiting and wondering, 'Why are they keeping me here for so long and when my torture comes, will I give up?' But I made a decision that I was prepared to die rather than bring someone else in here as well.

I was prepared for suicide. I'd rather die by my own hand, to die with dignity. I had two options: the mattress had metal things I could use to cut my wrists or if that didn't work I could break a glass. I had plans in place.

I didn't want to die, I had a strong sense of survival. I was in that nightmare and I wanted to get out of there. That was pure hell, knowing that all these human beings were doing these things as part of their normal job and some enjoy it. At the end of the day they go back to their wives and kids. How can they finish a shift of torturing someone and then go home to their children?

I could hear the sounds of the city from where I was, with people going to work and to school and I was locked in there enduring that nightmare and nobody knew. It's how I would describe hell.

Then one day they came and prepared me for a trip. I thought this was it, I was going to be dropped in the sea. By the sounds I could hear we were going into the city. They took me out of the car and walked me into a courtroom. That was a big surprise. I had a sense of hope that I was going be involved in some sort of legal process.

I found out then that I had been in a famous concentration camp called Cuatro Alamos, which means four cedars.

In the court they had a huge list of charges: illegal communication, trying to destabilise the elected government, lots of things. It's amazing how many charges they came up with for a peaceful twenty-one-year-old writing a pamphlet about democracy.

My family was there but not my husband – we'd separated before I was imprisoned. My mother told me she had been looking everywhere for me. They had denied that I'd been arrested. They told her I'd run away with a boyfriend.

They sentenced me to ten years' imprisonment for writing about human rights. I was sent to a women's prison where I had to share beds and tables with women who had chopped their husbands into little pieces, burnt down their houses with the kids inside and so on. I knew I had been disappeared.

I was there for a month or two and then they transferred me to a prison in my home town where I stayed for nearly a year.

By this time it was 1978 and Chile was under strong international pressure and had been threatened with an economic blockade. The people of Chile were attempting to create a revolution in peace and democracy.

With money sent from overseas we were able to get lawyers to defend us and they found a loophole in the law where you could exchange a prison sentence for exile. So I went for it and it was approved.

The day before I was going to be kicked out of the country they took me to say goodbye to my family. I was ready and packed to go. England had offered me refuge and a scholarship to continue my university studies, but then one of the prison guards came in with a newspaper and told me an amnesty had been decreed and we were all free because of the international pressure.

I stayed in the country for about another five months and joined the resistance once more. I was still being called into the police barracks for interrogation. Sometimes they followed me – you're always looking over your shoulder and your nerves become very frail, and I knew with the file I had that the next time I got arrested I would be shot on the spot.

One day they stopped a bus I was travelling on and it was searched. I thought they were looking for me – I nearly died. I was sweating and shaking, but they didn't find who they were looking for. I knew I couldn't do it any more. I went into a breakdown, paranoia basically, with justified reasons.

I went to London at the age of 22. I had never been on a plane before. I couldn't speak the language and knew nobody. And that was the start of another journey, the journey of life in exile. I came to Australia in 1986. I couldn't wait to get away from England with its cold weather and cold people.

Now I go back to Chile every five years to see my family. There are still people in prison there from that dictatorship; some have been there for over 25 years. There are still mothers who search the country for their children.

How it feels to be raped by a woman

Taylor, female, 34

❝ I had met this woman, Jess, through mutual friends and she seemed really nice. My last relationship had recently broken up and I was feeling quite lonely and keen to make new friends. Jess invited me to go out to dinner and I was really pleased and looking forward to it.

I thought it was strange that she insisted we meet at her house before heading out for the night, but it never crossed my mind that I might be in any danger; I thought she just wanted to show me her home.

Her house was in a really remote area and it was very dark outside because there were no streetlights. Anyway we had a drink and a chat and then she started showing me around. When we went into her bedroom she closed the door behind us and I was immediately alarmed.

She pushed me down on the bed. She was a big woman and much stronger than me. She started kissing me and

155

tried to get my clothes off. She was rubbing her face against mine and touching me all over. She said, 'If you just relax you'll enjoy this.'

I was in terrible shock, my mind racing. I'd never in my wildest dreams thought I could ever be in danger of assault from another woman.

She was pinning me down hard on the bed and shouting, 'I'm not letting you go until you have sex with me.' I started crying really hard; I was very upset. She finally let me up because I was struggling so violently. She got up and was very angry and insulting towards me. I think she had expected me to give in to her.

I ran to the back door of the house and realised she had locked it. That terrified me. I knew I had to keep my wits about me or this was going to be very bad because we were in such a remote area.

I stood there crying and begging her to leave me alone, reasoning with her. I was frightened that I was going to be badly hurt or that she would tear all my clothes off me. I kept crying and telling her I wanted to go. Eventually she gave up, unlocked the door, and I got out of there.

It had never crossed my mind that I could be raped by a woman, that a woman would consider doing something like that. I hate to think what could have happened if I had a smaller frame and was less able to fight her off.

At the time I thought there was no point in reporting the attack. Who would believe that a woman had attacked me? My only regret about not speaking out is that she went on to do the same thing to someone else a few months later. I had a lucky escape and it certainly taught me to be more cautious about jumping into friendships in the future.

157

How it feels to be drug-addicted and homeless

Janice Schilds, 41

66 **I became homeless** when I was about thirty-seven. I had a family with three children. I had a home, I had clothes on my back, I had money, I had my own business, but I was in full blown addiction, taking amphetamines. My situation was pretty bad; people were starting to talk and my business was going downhill. My relationship had been abusive and dysfunctional, so I had separated.

I'd started drinking and doing the teenage partying thing at about nineteen. My first relationship was with a dealer. There's always been drugs around me and it just went on from there.

At the start it was just a weekend plaything. By my thirties we were dabbling in and selling amphetamines. I knew I liked speed the moment I tried it – it made me feel normal; I felt good. When there was no money in dope we sold speed. For nine years I sold the stuff, while for me the drugs momentum was picking up.

I was using during the week but I wasn't IV-ing then – I was either putting it in a drink or snorting it. It wasn't until I left that relationship that the trouble really started. I thought that I could do the single mother thing and run a business on my own.

By 1999 I was IV-ing and in full blown addiction; I didn't realise how bad it was until people started to move away from me. That year I went into rehab for the first time. Going into rehab meant dropping absolutely everything in my life, and I couldn't do that, so I left and went back home to shut my business down. That's when I let my two children go; I let them live with their father. I told him that within a year I would be fine. Telling him I was sick was very difficult. I kept trying to detox but I would never stay in a clinic. I would always try to do it at home and that would last from nine to thirteen days. I was going mad, was doing weird things, crying, having fits of anger, isolating myself; my emotions were just out of whack.

My life became totally unmanageable in every respect. I lost my kids, I lost my family, my business, my home. The only thing that I held onto was my car and I've still got that today – it doesn't go, but I've still got it.

I was never to get those kids back. In a year I was worse and I was in denial. I had so much shame that I couldn't face my two kids. I wanted them to see me clean; I didn't want them to see what I had become.

Giving up my children was the hardest thing because I had to admit that I had a problem. I fought it to the end, I didn't think I had a problem, but then when I really had to stop using, I couldn't.

When I think of the lies that I told; the bullshit that I put my children through – late getting to school, not being there when they came home, being at my dealer's house and coming home an hour late to find them really pissed with me because there was nothing to eat. And there was no love and there was no food on the table and I would just shrug it off and say, 'Oh sorry, it won't happen again,' but I kept on saying the same thing.

When the kids left I went back into rehab again and I got turfed – told to leave – they said I could come back in two weeks if I was still clean. By that time my house was full of misfits – they took over my house. They were using very heavily and I knew I couldn't go back home because when I did I knew I'd use.

I was living in my car. I would sleep in car parks near my program. I would park near the Narcotics Anonymous rooms so I could get to a meeting. Then I was staying in my car in front of people's houses – even strangers – because then I'd feel safe.

I went to the nuns and asked if I could stay. I said, 'I need help, I've got nowhere to go.' They let me stay there and tried to keep me clean until it was time to go back to rehab. The next time I stayed for seven weeks and then I got turfed again, because I snuck out and used. I was very wilful, very naughty. So then I really had nowhere to go. I was basically in my car, doing the soup kitchens and other charities.

When I used I didn't care where I was or how I was living. When I was trying to get clean I was humiliated to have nowhere to go; it was the depths of despair really, but I was so adamant that I could do this. I really had the desire to stop using. I would go to any lengths just to get clean.

I lived in my car for about six months. It was freezing, I had a duvet and some clothes in my boot. The people I dealt with were addicts and they used me and my car to take drugs. So my car took a bit of a bashing at times, but I was so desperate for company and friends I didn't really care who they were so long as I didn't have to be alone. It was sad. I knew there had to be something better.

I did what I had to do to eat, to survive. I had to make money, I had to get some money. I knew there were ways and means. Girls worked the streets. I hated it. The couple of jobs that I did I gave the money to the nuns to look after and said, 'Only give me enough for a day, not enough to be able to buy drugs.'

When my car became unregistered I put it in a friend's garage and then I was completely homeless. I didn't have a lot of friends because I had walked away from most of my past.

I was homeless until the Salvation Army called me up and said I could join their Towards Independence program, and that was the one that worked for me. They got me back on my feet, they showed me how to budget my money, they put a roof over my head – first in a block of flats where you stay for seven weeks, then you go into independent housing for three months; then I was on my own. My caseworker from the Salvos still works with me; they've never let go of me completely. She helped me get Red Shield housing and that's what I've got now. I still try to go to NA meetings every day.

To stop using I had to think: 'Just don't pick up.' It's not easy to stop, but I had nothing more to lose, it was all gone, yet I had everything to gain if I stayed clean.

The lowest point was not having my kids, realising what I'd become and knowing that I was completely fucked. Many times on the streets I just sat back and thought: 'How the hell did this happen?' because it happened so fast, it made my head spin. It can happen to anyone.

By the time I got my shit together which was about twelve months later, and I went home, all my furniture was sold, my clothes were gone, the rent hadn't been paid, squatters had graffitied the walls. All my bank accounts had been drained because through addiction I trusted people to go to the bank for me.

It was near-on impossible to get off drugs, off the streets and back to a normal-sort of life. I did a lot of praying. I have a higher power in my life that works for me; you've got to have faith and believe in yourself and that it's going to get better – and it has.

I've been clean from my drug of choice for over three years; it got dangerous for me because I was starting to use heroin, and you can pick up a habit within a week. I was popping pills, taking anything to kill the pain. Everything seems OK when you're stoned, but then you've gotta come down off the shit and that's hard.

Life's still not the greatest. I have two more kids from a new relationship I thought was going to last forever. My youngest child was only three months when the bastard walked out the door to a Fleetwood Mac concert and never came back. I've been struggling with that for ages.

I suffer with depression, I suffer terribly and I'm on medication to give me some sort of balance. A lot of drug takers end up being depressed because they don't know how to cope with life without the use of some sort of mind-altering substance.

I don't think society wants to know about homeless people. I see junkies and homeless people on the street and my heart goes out to them. I wish that I had the strength and the facilities to help these people. Society doesn't care; people only want to know what's going on in their backyard.

I get to see my other two kids nearly every weekend now. I've built up a wonderful relationship with these kids. My daughter remembers everything – the lies, deceit, dysfunction, the craziness – but because I've worked to get to this point they respect me. I never gave up on myself totally. There was something inside me that said, 'You're a good person, you can do better, you can do better. You've just got to work, you've just got to push yourself to do it' – and I did.

How it feels to lose everything in a bushfire

Simon Poynton, 34

The whole day felt a bit ominous – the birds were acting strange and everyone felt a bit odd. The whole energy of the kids and the teachers at school was rather weird. The day was stinking hot and very, very windy. We heard over the radio that there were bad fires around and we could see the sky was getting darker. It looked like a dust storm but with smoke everywhere.

I felt pretty nervous knowing the fires were around because I'd already been through thirteen evacuations in ten years. We'd done it plenty of times, but luckily those fires were brought under control. People who live in the bush know that bushfires are a risk and that you have to be prepared.

We got home from school and pretty soon the place started to fill up with smoke. You could hear a gentle roar

165

in the background, almost like humming. We realised that this one was going to be a big one. No one came around, no police or fire brigade to tell us to evacuate – we just thought we'd better.

We grabbed a few things. I grabbed my golliwog Tuesday, my coin collection, and we legged it out of the house. I forgot my camera and I cried over that for ages because I'd just got into photography and had been given a little Instamatic which was my pride and joy. Losing my camera was a big issue for me and is something I still think about because now I am a photographer.

My dad was a wood craftsman, so he grabbed a few tools while Mum, my sister Ruth and I jumped in the car and headed down to the beach. There was a high cliff with a 220-yard walk to the water.

We had our two cats, Dudley and Toshka, with us and realised that we didn't have any drinking water for them or for us, so Ruth ran back to the house and got a container of water. My dad was still there and he told her to get out because part of the house was on fire.

We all stood huddled together in a circle in the sea – we spent four and a half hours like that. The water was up to my chest. I held one cat, Ruth held the other, and our parents held us. We had wet towels over our heads because the flames came right down to the sand. The waves kept crashing over us because they were so high from the wind. There were embers flying around everywhere and it was very hard to breathe. I had black boogers in my nose for months after that.

You couldn't see a thing. Every now and then you'd poke your head through the towels but all you could see was flames glowing. The sound was just ferocious – it was like a jet engine, but constant, just enormous. In the background we could hear explosions as people's gas cylinders from their barbecues and so on were blowing up.

It felt like the end of the world; we were very distraught emotionally. I think I was squeezing half the life out of the cat and I remember being clawed by it because cats don't like water, but mostly they were very good. They both let out a painful 'miaow' at one stage and I remember thinking that was when our house was engulfed.

We didn't know whether anyone else was in the water because we couldn't hear them or see them, but later we discovered that another guy was in the water with his dog about 300 feet away.

It was boiling hot in the water because we were only about forty feet from the fire. If we hadn't had the towels over our heads we would have got our hair singed. It was horrific – something I don't ever want to experience again.

The wind was so strong it was whipping the towels off us and we had to really hold them on. We didn't speak – it was too loud with the roar of the fire and the noise of the wind, and I think we were all in too much shock. We were doing everything we could do to survive – it was a life-or-death situation. But it gave us a sense of security knowing we were surrounded by water.

Four and a half hours later the fire front had passed and you could see it in the distance, heading towards Geelong, though everything around us was still burning.

We ventured back towards the car, but all the stairs in the side of the cliff were burning. Ruth had lost a sandal so she had to hop while we held on to her. The land was literally red hot after the ferocity of the fire. Afterwards it took a long time for seeds to germinate because it was such a hot fire; they reckon it burnt down to about twelve inches.

A fire engine came up the road and told us that one of the local milk bars was open and had sandwiches for any survivors. We went down there to get water and food – it was about 10.30 p.m. Going down the road we came within sight of our house and, when we turned, I said, 'Oh look, the neighbours' house didn't survive!' but in actual fact I was looking at the space where our house had been. I looked over and saw our chimney, and that was all that was left of the house.

I'd spent my whole life there yet there were no features left that I could identify – no landmarks of any sort were left. All the big trees that we knew and climbed, the power pole beside the house, were gone. I'd lost my bearings completely. It wasn't until we went past the empty block that I realised: 'This is it.'

We went back to the shop but it was closed. We got in anyway and just slept on the floor. It was pure and utter emotional exhaustion; it was like: Let's try to rest and see what we can deal with tomorrow.

In the morning we looked out of the window and it was like pictures I'd seen of Hiroshima, with a few buildings half standing and all these black sticks that were trees with no foliage. That was exactly what it was like. The ash made the whole ground grey. The amazing thing was that here and there was a house that had survived. That was just amazing. That's when you start to think: 'Why me? Why did that house survive and not ours?'

We had a look at what was left of Airey's Inlet and there was basically nothing – maybe three houses out of several hundred. We couldn't recognise anything; there was enormous open space because all the bush was gone and you could see right through where the trees used to be.

The air was still smoky. We got into where our house had been and I remember sitting down at the end of where my bed once was. I used to collect marbles, but all I found was a pile of fused glass. The ground was still so hot that the bottoms of my sneakers were melting and my feet were starting to burn.

Everyone was in their room, squatting down to see if there was anything left. My mum found some jewellery, which was all melted together. My sister is planning to make us each a pendant from that gold, like a phoenix coming out of the ashes.

It was complete shock, disbelief.

A month after Ash Wednesday my parents split up. I think the fire was the straw that broke the camel's back. Their history was wiped out in one sense; there were no shared belongings to hold onto any more.

The Salvation Army was fantastic at that time – they were the only reason we survived. They gave us clothes. One guy continued to visit us for about five years afterwards.

I didn't get any counselling and it all hit home about two years later when I was about fifteen. I used to sit on the end of my bed and cry with a razor blade held to my wrists. The only thing that kept me going was the thought that people would believe I'd given in.

It took a long time to get over it and I think every twelve or eighteen months it would surface again and I had to deal with a little bit more. I did that for ten years, I reckon. Now, having dealt with it, I see it as just one of those things, but I do really enjoy my material possessions because once I lost them all.

How it feels to have an organ transplant

Jason Grey

I was diagnosed with cystic fibrosis at nine months of age. Until I was twelve I had no troubles whatsoever. Then I started getting stomach pains and stomach problems and I had to go into hospital to have a bile-duct bypass.

Then everything went fine until I was about seventeen or eighteen – that's when I started to notice things were a little bit more difficult. I was getting short of breath, having trouble doing things and being admitted to hospital more often.

One Christmas when I was 21 I got really sick and just didn't recover. I was in bed for about three or four weeks. Then I went to hospital and had some antibiotics for the chest infection, but I had left it too long and it had taken over my whole body. We finally got it sorted out but I never returned to normal health. I just couldn't handle it any more. So I mostly stayed home. If I went out I had to plan ahead to ensure I'd be OK. I had to know if I would need to walk far, or if I was going to get worn out. I couldn't be spontaneous; life wasn't much fun.

By then I'd had the problem for 25 years and my lungs were deteriorating rapidly. I was frightened about dying. There were times when I felt as if I was on my deathbed and wondering if I would be here tomorrow. I'd think: 'There're so many things I haven't done – I'm so young.'

It was very frustrating because I'd feel fine one day and the next day couldn't get out of bed. And always thinking, 'Am I going to be OK tomorrow?'

There were times when I thought, 'Why me, why did it happen to me? I wish I could get rid of it' – all that sort of stuff.

My hospital stays became more frequent and in 2001 the doctor said, 'OK, it's time you thought about a transplant.' At that time I said, 'No, I don't want a transplant – that's the end of the world for me and I won't consider it.'

When people said the word 'transplant' I thought, 'Oh my God, that's the end for me; I'm going to die now.' No one ever explained that you have your transplant and you get a whole new life.

They put off talking about a transplant for a while, and then I got really, really sick again and they said, 'You've only got twelve or eighteen months to live; you really need to consider having the transplant.'

The doctors organised a meeting with my parents and me to talk about my fears and come to some sort of agreement. They gave me a few books to read. Hearing the stories of people who have had transplants does make you think that maybe it is possible for you.

I went to the hospital and I had some tests done to see if I was eligible for a transplant. But they said I had liver problems as well and that the CF was quite advanced, so if they were to try surgery I would probably die on the table. Liver disease is fairly common in people with CF.

They sent me back to my doctor to talk it over and he said there were some other options, and one was to see a specialist doctor, Keith McNeil, in Queensland and try for a triple transplant. They hadn't done any over here at that stage, though eight or nine had been done in England, and Dr McNeil had observed a lot of them.

I went to see him and he said I was the perfect candidate for heart, lung and liver transplant.

He told me to move to Queensland to be near the hospital, so a few months later my mother, brother and I moved. I went on the transplant list in late August and the waiting began. It was about nine or ten months before I got the call. That was probably the hardest part. Every day the phone rings and you wonder if it's the hospital. There are days when you think, 'Is it ever going to happen? Will it happen in time?'

In the meantime I was going back and forth to hospital. I had a couple of collapsed lungs and some internal bleeding. When you get those episodes, that's when you think, 'This is looking bad now.'

I was in hospital with a collapsed lung when the call finally came. I was lying in bed at about eight-thirty one night. Dr McNeil came in, put his hand on my feet and said, 'We may have an organ for you; nothing's confirmed. Hang tight and I'll be back in a minute.'

I rang Mum, and a couple of nurses came in and gave me a hug. Mum was there in five or ten minutes. I felt a whole heap of mixed emotions; I was scared and relieved at the same time. I didn't know what to expect or what would happen next. My head was running a million miles an hour.

The doctor came back about half an hour later and said the surgeons were on their way and the organs were organised, although they would take a couple of hours to reach us. I had some blood tests, some tablets and a scrub-down. By the time all that was done about three hours had passed and I was ready to go to surgery.

It was just like: 'It's happening, this is it.' I did think that it could be the end.

The surgery took fifteen hours, and when I came out I had internal bleeding and had to go back a couple of times.

I woke up in ICU recovery and everyone was there – that was excellent. I was sore and out of it, but when you get to see those people standing around the bed, you think, 'Yes! I've come through it.' It's an incredible feeling.

Three days later they took the breathing tube out and those first few breaths were the weirdest – it's like you have to learn to breathe again. I'd become so used to taking short shallow breaths that when I got these new lungs I was almost hyperventilating. Having brand new lungs that could breathe was very strange. It took a week or two to get used to it. Being able to take a big breath was excellent – it took me about a month to realise how deeply I could breathe and how good it felt.

I was in hospital for seven weeks and I was scared at first to come home. I didn't know whether I'd be safe with these new organs. Once I got used to it, it was great. I could hang out with my friends and do what I wanted to do and not have to worry about whether I had enough oxygen. It was life-changing.

I still have CF but it doesn't affect these new lungs or liver; it won't re-infect.

I used to have physio twice a day. Now I don't have to do so much and that feels fantastic.

Now after a year I'm doing great, I haven't had any problems. My brother has CF and so does his girlfriend and they go into hospital every now and again, so that's hard. His girlfriend is on the transplant list at the moment.

All my three organs came from one person. It doesn't feel weird to have someone else's lungs, liver and heart – the only difference is that I can breathe now.

I've heard stories about people who have had transplants and say they take on characteristics of their donor, like – you know, 'I never used to like beer, but now I like it.' But I haven't noticed anything like that. My tastebuds may have changed a bit but I think that's just because of the drugs I'm taking.

I don't know anything about the donor. I feel truly sad for their family, but I'm grateful for what that family did and what they've given me – a whole new lease on life. I'm just really, really happy that they agreed to donate. I'm over the moon about it.

How it feels to stop a serial killer

David

I was coming home from work in north-east Victoria in the late eighties. My workmate was driving and was anxious to get back so he could go to the pub.

As we came up to the Ovens River Bridge I noticed a bicycle partially obstructing the narrow country bridge. My immediate thought was that some accident had just happened, because the back wheel on the bicycle was still spinning.

There was no one in sight but I told my mate to stop the car. At that stage two people came out from behind some bush on the side of the bridge. It was a man of about thirty-five years. He had his arm around the shoulders of a young girl of about ten or twelve.

I said, 'Are you all right?' The young girl opened her mouth; she didn't say anything, but there was blood in her mouth. I found out in hindsight that he was waiting on the bridge and punched her off the bicycle.

I said, 'What's going on?' He looked at me and said, 'She'll be all right, mate, she'll be all right.' He was holding her quite firmly. We didn't know it then, but he had a knife stuck under her jacket in her armpit. I knew that this was very serious,

I could feel the intensity and the emotion.

A couple other cars were waiting to cross the bridge. In the first car was an elderly couple who pulled up and asked what was going on.

Sally, the young girl, then screamed at the top of her lungs and said, 'He's attacked me, he's trying to attack me.'

He let the young girl go and ran towards his car which was parked down near the river. I realised the girl was safe, so I ran back to a vehicle on the side of the road; it was another mate of ours on his way home from work. I said, 'Billy, that guy's attacked that young girl.' He roared off in his four-wheel-drive to chase him.

Not far from the bridge there was a Y-intersection and in the middle of it was a gravel pit with lots and lots of blackberries and shrubs. The offender ran into that to hide.

I went back to my vehicle and called for assistance on the two-way. I said, 'If you can hear me, phone the police. There's been a girl attacked.' I then drove the car as far as I could into the bush where the guy had gone.

By this stage several people had come around and we realised we had him trapped in the bush. Another guy, Johnny, and an elderly farmer were standing on one road and they had a rifle to stop him. I went up another way and the local apple farmers were guarding the road there. The elderly couple were comforting the young girl, she was screaming and screaming.

There were a few of the lads in this gravel pit in the middle of the intersection, throwing rocks at him. They were trying to flush him out of the blackberries but he was hiding underneath the bushes. You could tell exactly where he was though because the tops of the blackberries were wiggling.

I was opening the back door of my car to get some tools to defend myself when he sprang up out of the bushes straight in front of me. That's when I spotted the big hunting knife. It was an eight- or ten-inch blade.

He was running perpendicular to me with the weapon in his hand but he was fleeing, not trying to attack me.

He took off into the scrub and a young lad and I gave chase and were right on his tail but felt a bit intimidated by his knife, so we stopped and grabbed a couple of big rocks and continued after him.

We chased him through the bush and every time he looked like turning around I yelled out, 'Shoot him, blow his leg off!'

We almost caught up to him as he was crawling through a barbed-wire fence. We were getting closer and closer and I was about to let my big rock go, but I thought, 'I've got to save these because I might really need them.'

He turned at that point and looked me square in the eyes. I just kept screaming at the top of my lungs, 'Blow his leg off, shoot him, shoot him!' just to bluff him, because I wanted to keep him going in the other direction. I knew that we were heading towards a farmhouse and I thought that if we could corner him in one of the buildings we'd be OK. We'd rallied a lot of support and I knew that the police had been called so we were well on our way to getting him.

He ran through the yard of one of Victoria's most prominent High-Plains cattlemen. There seemed to be 100 dogs tied up on chains and several horses. As the offender ran through he woke up all the dogs and horses and I was jumping sideways to avoid getting bitten.

The cattleman – in his late seventies and a real rugged character – came out of his shed and said, 'What the fuck's going on here?' and I said, 'Mr Blair, that man's attacked a girl; grab your gun.'

So we kept chasing and chasing – it seemed like eternity to me. We broke into an open paddock and I was really frightened that he was going to get away. I didn't think I could run up to the top of the hill in front of us, I was buggered. The whole time I was chasing him I was screaming at the top of my lungs – the entire time, just to intimidate him.

I was starting to feel disheartened but then I heard the coppers pull into the paddock behind us and the senior sergeant yelled, 'Give it up, mate, or you'll regret it,' and then they were running beside me.

That's when the fellow gave up. He threw the knife into the creek and then he lay down in the bush. The police turned on me. They were shouting, 'Get away, get away now,' because I was making these bloodcurdling screams at him, but it was all bluff. I was mentally and physically exhausted.

I don't know why it was so important for me to catch him; it just meant a lot to me that he should pay for what he'd done.

Later during the interview the coppers asked him, 'What where you going to do with the girl?' and he said, 'What girl? There was no girl.' So they said, 'Well why were you running?' and he said, 'I thought that mad bastard with the beard was going to kill me.' He was frightened to death by me but it was fear that was fuelling my ferocity – I was frightened to death that he was going to turn around and stick the knife between my ribs.

I met the girl's father shortly afterwards and he was very appreciative and thankful. He was just devastated by the whole thing. She was a very robust girl and at the time didn't seem to have suffered too badly from the assault, but later she really fell apart. She was very distressed.

He got four years for attacking her. Then the police told me that he had done time for raping another woman, had stabbed her several times, strangled her with her bra and thrown her off the bridge into the water. She regained consciousness in the cold water and crawled to safety. They felt very certain that he'd also done another attack in which the victim was killed.

I was a bit nervous that he might get out of jail and come looking for me, but the police said it wouldn't happen.

Four or five years later I saw an article in a paper about him. The headline said something like 'serial killer never to walk the streets' and it said this man had been terrorising women all the way up the east coast of Australia. The article was very detailed and Sally was on the front page. That was when I learned that he'd been put away for life.

I took the article home and it sat on my bench for weeks, but I never, ever read it. I looked at it one day and the tears welled up in my eyes and I thought, 'This arsehole has taken so much from so many people, but he's not going to take anything from me, I can't spend the rest of my life thinking about what he did to those girls.' So I burnt it. I didn't want to know. But it will always be with me.

I don't really have any feelings of pride about catching him. I just think the whole thing is so awful and negative I'm thankful that he's not on the streets any more.

'**THE BEST THING ABOUT HAVING THEM
IS THAT IT'S FIVE TIMES EVERYTHING**'

How it feels to have quintuplets

Adele Chapman-Burgess, 44

❝ **We'd been trying** to have a baby for ten years. We'd done three cycles of IVF and then tried the GIFT program. Every time a cycle failed I vowed never to put my body through it again. I thought I was never going to have a baby. Then on the third GIFT cycle I pretty much knew I was pregnant straightaway.

When they do the egg transfer they only put in three because that's their ethical quota.

I was so sick I couldn't get out of bed. We knew three eggs had been put back so my local doctor said I was probably having more than one baby. The thought of having three didn't faze us.

I had a scan a week later and the assistant said, 'How many eggs did you have put back?' We told her and she said, 'Well, I can count five. Look, I'll show you.' They looked like a little bunch of grapes. Then she went and

183

got the head guy and he came in and was absolutely blown away. There're only four sets of quintuplets in Australia.

I was lying down at the time – which was good. My husband Bert was sitting beside me, squeezing my hand and saying, 'Five, five! How could this happen?' and he's squeezing my hand harder and harder.

They gave us a photo and we got in the car and drove to the parking lot at Pizza Hut and just sat there contemplating what it all meant. It was way beyond anything we'd ever imagined. We were speechless.

I rang my mum and she just laughed and said, 'Well, you wanted a baby.' I said, 'Yes, but I didn't want five babies!'

I was in shock, I didn't know what we were going to do, and she said, 'We'll just take it one day at a time and deal with what comes; we'll get through this, it'll be all right.'

I thought: 'That's all right for you to say – you don't have to carry five babies.'

We have no idea how we ended up with five babies. The hospital had to recall all the nursing staff, doctors and technicians to go through all the paperwork and check that there were no mistakes. But they couldn't explain what happened. We think either they'd left a couple of eggs in there from a previous cycle or maybe there were already some eggs in the fallopian tubes. It was something they couldn't explain. Those were obviously two very determined babies.

I was worried all the way; at every single stage, at every given moment there could have been something that went wrong. We worried about conjoined babies, or a child with Down Syndrome. I had a bit of a bleed and the doctors were worried that I might lose one. In fact there was a possibility that we did lose one, that there were originally six.

The doctors said to take it steady with everything and not do too much. They told me if I wanted to have all these babies I just had to be the incubator. And that wasn't a hard decision to make, after waiting ten years for a baby. When such an opportunity comes along, you don't risk anything. We made lots of sacrifices and had a fantastic support system around us.

We live in a little country town in New South Wales, so word got out pretty quickly that we were having quins and the support was fabulous. The town thinks they own the children.

Some people were a bit negative, saying, 'You'll be lucky if you get one baby out of this.' We had to go through a lot of things like that, but we decided only to surround ourselves with positive thoughts.

At 24 weeks I flew up on an air-ambulance to the hospital in Brisbane. I had a member of my family with me at all times and people calling in for the whole two months I was there.

The staff kept saying, 'Keep the babies in; you're doing really well.' At about 32 weeks they were amazed that I was still going. They had a paediatrician, the head nurse and two other nurses per baby scheduled to be in the operating theatre. The whole team was on tenterhooks because they had agreed to be on call for the birth. For two months those guys were living on the edge, waiting for a phone call.

At 32 weeks I was getting edgy and also huge. My stretch marks were starting to weep, and until then I'd had constant movement from the babies, then all of a sudden they stopped. I got a bit worried and stressed, so the hospital decided it was time. I carried the babies for 32 weeks and six days, the longest quintuplet gestation in Australia.

I had an epidural, which took an hour to administer. There was a lot of tugging and carrying on and then – there was the first baby, Jack. He peed all over the doctor. All of them came out fine and healthy.

The second one was Louis. For the next I was pleading, 'Please be a girl, just give me one girl.' And they pulled out Erika, so yes! I got a girl. The next one was India and the last one was Georgia.

I had to have ten names ready because we didn't know the sex of the babies, but I had plenty of time to do it. Because we are of Aboriginal descent we chose Aboriginal names for their second names.

The babies all got whipped off quite quickly. As soon as Jack came out he was named 'Jack Jardie', which means 'firstborn boy'. The next one that went past us, we said, 'That's Louis.' At first my husband didn't like the name 'India', but as she was going past – this little baby with masses and masses of dark hair – he said, 'That's India,' so that was it. The other two took a few days to decide.

Not one of the babies needed to go into the special-care nursery or humidicrib. Jack was in an oxygen box for twenty-four hours. He was the biggest at four pounds and half an ounce. India was the smallest – she was just three pounds and half an ounce. My placenta weighed something like twenty pounds.

When I was pregnant I never thought about holding the babies. You stay away from that. We didn't put a nursery together. Everything was left until we could bring them home. We didn't want to let our barriers down, just in case.

They came home to our little housing-commission house three weeks before their due date. That day I took their armbands off because Bert and I knew which was which, and by that afternoon we could recognise their cries.

We asked for volunteers to come into the house and soon we had people in our house 24/7. Our last volunteer would leave at 10 p.m. and the next would be back at 6 a.m.

The local social worker fought tooth and nail to get us a nurse for the first 16 weeks. There were times when I wanted to walk away from being so full-on all the time. I didn't want to walk away from the babies, but it was very hard never having any privacy. I had 40 volunteers a week with us around the clock until the babies were about six months old. From then until the babies were two, we had volunteers from morning until 6 p.m. Then people who just wanted to be with the children because they loved them would come on Saturday mornings right up until they were three or four years old.

But it got easier as they got older and the best thing about having them is that it's five times everything. You only have to know how much joy one baby gives to you – then multiply that by five.

When the kids were in grade two, I went to university as a mature-age student and I graduated as a teacher last year.

They've just turned twelve and they all get on really well. This year we've got two school captains, one of the girls is on the Student Representative Committee and two others are house captains. It's starting to sink in to them that they're pretty special.

I believe God dishes out to people what he thinks they can handle.

How it feels to be caught in a cyclone

Peter Eves, 44

I'd had a small operation and was watching the news in hospital. I'd seen Cyclone Vance start off as a small low on the weather chart. I watched it for a few days, then eventually I said, 'I'm out of here,' and discharged myself to go home and pack up our gear.

We were operating a salvage business at the time. I knew that I wouldn't be able to do too much after the operation, so on the way home I picked up a hitchhiker and offered him some work helping me to prepare.

With cyclones you have good warning; they don't just pop up in the middle of the night. This was the worst really bad one we've had. We've been here in Exmouth, Western Australia, for ten years and there've been about four that have come close to us. The longer you live here, the better the odds get in their favour.

A lot of people pack up and leave, but what do you do then? At that time we had no prediction of where the cyclone was heading. It was the luck of the draw – it could have gone on the outside of us; it could have turned off and gone elsewhere.

It's pretty frightening knowing a cyclone is on its way. A lot of people were very nervous and very jittery and for quite a time afterwards the wind would blow and you'd hear that whistling noise and the hairs would stand up on the back of your neck.

The night before it hit we were listening to news reports and tracking it on maps. We were getting rain and winds of about forty miles an hour, just strong enough to be uncomfortable.

Exmouth was originally built by the US Navy; they build their houses with a lot of concrete – concrete walls and concrete roof. Fortunately we've got one of those on either side of our house and two behind us. One was vacant at the time; it was a holiday house belonging to the police union. I got in touch with the police and asked if we could move there for shelter if things got bad because we were in a thirty-year-old fibro-and-timber house. Like the three little pigs, you always go to somewhere stronger.

My wife Vicky and the two kids moved over the night before and I stayed home till the next morning. There's not much sleep. You're listening to the forecasts and thinking about the cleaning up you didn't get time to do.

I woke up at about 5 a.m. and the wind was really starting to scream, so I grabbed a few more things and started moving them across to the other house. By 8 a.m. she was fairly humming.

The eye of the cyclone passed here about 10 a.m. Then the wind changed, the eye crossed very close to us and the wind came from a different direction. As the eye came closer we got what's called a 'white-out'. The rain is driven so hard that you could open the back door but see only about three metres ahead. It's like a snowstorm, but it's just rain travelling hard and fast.

The wind was a roar, it just screamed. I've never heard anything like it. You're hearing things banging off the wall and off the roof. Our house was next-door and we heard a couple of big thumps, and I thought we'd lost the house.

The sky was just totally black; it was almost like night because the cloud is so intense there's no light. When the eye of the cyclone hits, you get a bit of light – it comes up like a dawn glow for a short time.

At that stage it created the strongest winds ever recorded in the Southern Hemisphere; the official speed was 166 miles an hour.

At about 2 p.m. it subsided enough for us to go outside. We went walking around, looking at everything. The damage was quite incredible. There wasn't a leaf in town – well, not on the trees anyway – they were plastered all over people's walls and floors. Our house, which survived, was full of them because the windows and doors had

191

blown open, so the inside of the house was full of debris. Instead of foliage, the trees all had tin leaves – bits of scrap metal and aluminium.

There were no deaths. There were a few injuries, but no one was seriously hurt. One lady got stuck underneath her house for six hours after it collapsed and she sat there singing hymns all night.

There were quite a few houses lost. We lost our business premises and a lot of gear; we had to start from scratch. The cyclone blew all the walls away; everything that was inside got thrown around and turfed out. The SES (State Emergency Services) turned up to help us with the cleanup, and did in a few hours what would have taken me days on my own. All that Vicky and I could do was hug each other and cry with relief and sadness.

We had lots of personal items stored at the business – photo albums, books, and so on, which we lost. Vicky lost her silver tea service and was pretty upset about that, but one day she was out walking and found the sugar pot lying in the mud.

The other premises, which I was building, lost all its doors. We found one huge door 500 yards away. One set of doors we never found at all – they're probably out at sea.

The town, which has about 2,500 people, lost its water supply. Over here we've got American-style water hydrants that stick up from the ground. A caravan got blown along the street and knocked a hydrant over and that drained our two tanks of water.

We lost our electricity and phone lines too and didn't get anything back for about two weeks. We had no services.

Everybody just went camping in their houses. It was still raining so you filled up whatever you could with water and used it to flush the toilet and to drink. Everybody just showered under the run-off from the roof. It was back-to-basics but no one really worried.

The biggest drama was getting the kids away. It took a couple of days to get that organised. Because we had no water or power it became a health issue, so we sent them to their grandparents.

We had water and supplies flown in on Air Force Hercules and they then took people out – mainly tourists and women and children – but it took days. The rest of us stayed in town because we had to clean up.

After a few days the Council went around with a big skip – we called them the 'Pong Squad' – and made everyone empty the contents of their freezers because of the danger of rotting food.

This sort of thing really brings out the best and worst in people and a community. The f-word really became the word in town. We were all just walking around, looking at the devastation, saying, 'F…!' Even the little old ladies were doing the crow call. We were all stunned, with our eyes like saucers, but it was quite hilarious how all we could do was swear. Some people were so shell-shocked that they packed up and never came back.

How it feels to battle with cancer

Mark, 35

I'd lost lots of weight – about one and a half stone over eighteen months, but it didn't bother me too much. I thought it was because I was doing more work in the garden. For most of 2003 there were times when I was feeling lethargic and slightly flu-ish, but I never investigated why.

I also had shoulder pain. I thought it was maybe from using the computer too much. I told my GP in about June but he didn't make any connection with the symptoms of liver cancer, which it actually is.

There weren't many side-effects – it was originally bowel cancer that spread to the liver, so bowel movements had changed over a long period of time, but there was never any direct sign that something was really bad, no blood or anything.

In the middle of October for about four days in a row I had a pain low on my left side. I went to the GP and he checked me out more thoroughly. He ordered blood tests and an ultrasound.

The blood tests didn't reveal anything, but the ultrasound showed that there was something in my liver, something quite large on the right side. I had a CT scan straight away and that revealed a seven-centimetre tumour in my descending colon which was almost completely blocking it off, and also a four-inch-diameter tumour in my liver which occupied the whole right third of it.

It was worrying, though I still didn't think it would be cancer. But when I went back to the GP he started using these big words and I knew it was more serious. I had tears in my eyes when he was talking to me, and driving home I was very emotional and teary. Having to break the news to my wife and parents was hard.

It was all very, very quick. Only about two weeks from the tests to my being in hospital. There wasn't time to be mulling over everything, you're just in the doctors' hands and you do what you're told and go along with everything.

I thought that this could be a death sentence because there was a tumour in the liver as well as the bowel – though I knew that the bowel cancer was bad and had probably been there for quite a while judging from the size of it. There was also a worry about where else the cancer could have spread that wasn't showing up on the scans.

I was referred to a surgeon to have a colonoscopy, which wasn't successful because they couldn't get past the tumour.

I had surgery a week later to have the bowel cancer removed. I was in hospital for fifteen days because there was a complication after the initial surgery. My intestines had developed adhesions where they had been flattened, like a hose squashed together, so my digestive system wasn't working and I had to be opened up again a week later to fix that up. I lost a heap more weight and went down to about nine stone, so I looked pretty gaunt and awful. I felt sick and in pain the whole time I was in hospital.

It was a very painful and slow recovery and there was all that worry about not knowing the future. I focused on recovering from that surgery and blocking out any thought of the next operation in February. I was also told I'd be having chemotherapy afterwards.

I virtually couldn't do anything for two months during the recovery phase. It's extremely debilitating being cut down the middle; all those muscles control just about every move that you make and so I couldn't do much.

The extended family's worry about what was happening didn't get relayed to me until later on. I guess they were trying to be strong and not upset me. You do get upset talking about it, but actually talking would have helped. I would have liked to know how they were feeling or how my being this way, or maybe dying, was going to affect them. I wanted us all to be honest.

Some family members have been able to talk to me really truthfully and that's helped, but others have reacted by not knowing what to do. None of that bothered me; how people reacted to me didn't upset me. It was more my own feeling of: 'How many years have I got left? Or is it less than a year?' – that sort of thing.

I wondered how long I had to live and whether there was any point planning anything or whether I would miss the kids' growing up. It's the things I would lose by dying that upset me more than what other people said. Their being upset didn't upset me. Talking about how they would deal with this loss in the family was fine.

After the liver surgery I was in hospital for eight days; then I had to recover from that and start chemo.

Just before the chemo started I had another CT scan which showed some new spots in my liver and in my lung. That was really, really devastating. That was my lowest point. I went to see the surgeon and he mentioned other treatments, like lasers and so on. But it didn't sound very promising.

Already going through the two operations and recovering and then being told there was something else – that was certainly the worst thing I've been through – it was worse than the initial diagnosis. Going through all the pain and crap with the operations is one thing, but then to know that the pain and stress are going to linger on, and to have that anxiety on an ongoing basis is pretty upsetting.

I started the chemo and now I've done five cycles. I had another CT scan last week with a new machine that allows them to see 3D images. This showed that the tumour in my liver has got smaller and it might not be what they thought it was – and there was nothing in my lungs, so either the chemo is doing the job or you could even suspect that those images might have been scar tissue from earlier infections. So that was more positive news, especially that there were no new cancers.

It gives me hope that the chemo is working or that the other things aren't too serious yet, so that I have more time. I'll continue with the chemo and hopefully I'll have a bit of life left after that.

Even though the bowel cancer may have formed up to three years ago and the liver thing was probably there for a year and a half, I have not felt like blaming the doctors for failing to pick things up earlier, nor have I felt any anger. But I have had the 'why me?' feeling, because I don't smoke and I don't drink; I've led a pretty calm sort of life, and I eat sensibly – so it just seems really unlucky and unfair. When I talk to the oncologist, the way he describes things is that it's all about prolonging your life, rather than finding a cure.

I don't think cancer has changed me a great deal. Sex is something that bothered me – everything changed; you couldn't do what you wanted to do and felt ugly because of the scars and soreness. So that put me off.

My wife and I have talked about the future – like, if I do die, where I want to be buried and things like that, and how she'll manage financially. We want to have as much family time as possible – short holidays and things like that.

I have a lot of sadness about missing out on things in the future, missing out on life with my wife and kids and friends; thinking about things around the house and garden that might take years to do – and what's the point of that? You lose hope and it's hard to see yourself in the future.

How it feels when there is a murder in your family

David

It happened in 1973, two days before my sixteenth birthday. Maryanne was 24 when she was killed.

She had been married for three or four years, but there was a growing tension around her husband's sexuality and as a consequence they split up, though they remained on good terms.

A friend of a friend came to stay with them shortly before they split up; Maryanne and he became good friends and eventually lovers. He was a heroin addict and he either introduced her to heroin or promoted its use. But he was quite abusive, physically and verbally, and as a consequence they were only together for about three months before she told him to leave.

He continued to pester her though, and she felt quite vulnerable. But after he hadn't contacted her for a couple of weeks she believed that it was finally over.

Then he got himself high and went to her house with the intention of killing her. He had a gun with him, wrapped in a cloth. He put it in an outside toilet at Maryanne's house. Because it was a weekday, he assumed she was at school teaching. He must have gone into the house just to have a look around, but discovered that she was asleep in bed with the flu. So he went back out to the toilet for his gun. He shot my sister three times in the head and then shot himself in the heart.

The landlord came around at 5 p.m. that afternoon. He and Maryanne were good friends, and the backdoor was open, so he walked in. He found them in the bedroom with her lying in bed looking quite calm and peaceful because she was shot in her sleep, and him spread across the bed. It was obviously a horrific scene.

My family was told straight away but, because I was working on a dairy farm out of Melbourne, they didn't really know how to tell me. They decided one of the family should come and get me rather than tell me over the phone.

The morning after Maryanne was shot I was on the farm milking at six in the morning and a Mercedes pulled into the driveway. This was a most unusual thing on a dairy farm – for such a flash car to be there. I thought it must have been someone for the boss, so I just kept milking. The next thing, the boss tapped me on the shoulder and said, 'David, your sister's here.' It was my younger sister. I went over and gave her a hug. It felt rather strange because the family had never visited me on the farm. She took me into a room next to the dairy and told me that my elder sister had been shot and killed.

It was just the most surreal experience to be told in that environment – in the dairy with all the pumping machines going, and the cows… to find out that your sister's been murdered. The fact that she died a violent death was abhorrent.

I couldn't stand it.

I just went into shock. I was waiting for my sister to tell me it was a joke. It was 6 a.m., the dawn was just breaking, it was freezing bloody cold and there we were – me with my ten layers of clothes and gumboots, and cows mooing in the background, the dairy going full pelt, and my sister's telling me that our older sister was murdered yesterday.

I had this feeling of absolute disbelief. I remember trying to pack up my bag to leave and my sister's trying to be practical, saying, 'David, where are your underpants, where are your socks, what do you want to wear?' And I'm thinking to myself, 'I don't care if I wear underpants and nothing else,' because making decisions like that seemed to have no meaning at all. It just had no significance.

The funeral was about three days later. My mother was absolutely distraught. She wondered whether the way she had dealt with Maryanne's boisterous personality had had an impact on her death – or at least on her decisions.

Mum's never been the same since it happened. Even now, 31 years later, she is still given to more volatile emotions than most people – both sadness and joy. It's interesting, the scar that the murder has left on her. I don't think you could wish upon a parent any more terrible or traumatic incident than to lose a child. My mother just never really recovered. In those days counselling wasn't routine, so she was never offered any support.

The man who killed my sister, his parents were Canadian. The police told us that they had to send a report over to Canada and his body would be sent back there.

My mother asked if it was mandatory that his parents know he murdered her daughter and the police said not necessarily. So my mother insisted that, for the parents' sake, they not be told. To this day they have no idea. She said there was nothing to be gained by their knowing; it would only make them feel more distraught. It was such a generous suggestion.

Because Maryanne was nine or ten years older than myself, she was like a second mother to me. She was intriguing because she was from the seventies' art world. I used to stay with her and my brother-in-law quite often; it was like a home away from home, an escape from the tumultuous atmosphere at our house – because Dad was an alcoholic and his emotions were all over the place.

My family hadn't told me that the man who killed Maryanne was a heroin addict. When it did come out, there was no suggestion that Maryanne had also indulged. The last thing I would have believed was that she had been hooked on drugs or would have used a drug that I considered to be incredibly dangerous and counter-productive.

About a year after her death, my younger sister Robin told me that during the autopsy they found track marks on Maryanne's arms.

I remember sitting in the back of Robin's car and I cried from the time we left Geelong till we got to Melbourne. I just couldn't believe that my sister had used a drug like that – and that there was physical evidence she had used it more than once, indicating it wasn't just experimentation.

I then found out that one reason she broke up from the man was that she wanted to stop using. I'm sure she wanted to change her life, but he put a stop to that.

Her death is still a source of great sadness. Maryanne was a really great artist. I've no doubt that if she'd stayed alive, she could have been famous. She really was incredibly talented and very well respected as an artist. That alone fills me with sadness, that level of talent being wasted.

She was volatile but at the same time amazingly joyful. She had a fiery spirit and was a very funny person. She's often in my thoughts, and some of my personality traits are reflections of hers.

She would have brought joy to a lot of people and got a lot out of life herself. I often think, 'What would she be like now?' It's hard to imagine what she would have been like at 55.

I feel great anger towards the man who killed her. I find it difficult to forgive him for not exercising a greater level of control over his anger.

My mother is glad he killed himself because she wanted to kill him. I would have been after him for sure. Small as I was, I certainly would have been looking for him.

How it feels to be brainwashed by a cult

Luke, 34

In 1999 my wife Sally's doctor advised her to spend a few days with this group for respite care. She was suffering postnatal depression after having our second child.

The doctor didn't know anything about the community. She thought they were just really nice people. She didn't know they were actually a cult – and at that stage neither did we.

After the second day there my wife believed she was a sinner going to hell. The only hope she had was to give up everything and live there. She was ready to leave me and join. She didn't know anything about the group, but it filled some deep need within her. She was looking for something to make herself feel valuable.

I'm not sure if she would have taken the children with her or not at that stage. But the cult told her she had to come home and 'win me over' – to get me into it too.

206

That process would take about six months. Unknown to me, she told them I'd be bringing in about $400,000 to the community, so they were very keen to get me in and really used the big guns to persuade me. She was a bit unhinged – we had nothing like that amount of money.

I thought we had a fairly good marriage, I didn't know she was so desperately unhappy. She didn't appear to be, she didn't tell me that she was, but obviously the group provided something that was missing in her life.

So eventually we joined. I gave up my family business, giving it back to my father. I was doing contract manufacturing, producing chemical blends for customers. We sold our house and paid off the mortgage and had a big garage sale to sell all our possessions. Whatever was left we gave away. We went into the community with clothes and a few personal items.

We gave them around $12,000 to $13,000, which was everything we had. I convinced myself that we were doing the right thing. A lot of what they said made sense, but the big motivation for me was that I was pretty sure I'd lose Sally if I didn't join.

My parents were thoroughly pissed off because I didn't really talk to them about it. I sprang it on them, which was a sign that I wasn't really comfortable with the decision.

Once you join you have no car, no money – if you want to do anything you have to ask; if you want a new pair of underpants you've got to ask.

Each day you'd have no idea what you would be doing; you'd be rostered on for different jobs in the community. Being a qualified teacher I did some teaching in the mornings, and in the afternoons I would do manual labour – cutting lawns, digging trenches. I did a lot of driving – picking up and delivering things.

My wife and I moved into a room about sixteen feet by eleven feet wide, and then we had an extra room added for the kids. Everything else was shared by the whole community – bathrooms, toilets and kitchen.

Every day the community would have breakfast together; whoever was working together would have lunch as a group; and we'd all have dinner together.

Women took a very subservient role, except for those they called the 'Wise Women' – these had power. All the women had to dress modestly. They generally worked in the kitchen or the laundry – that's about it. My wife didn't have a problem with that.

If you were single you weren't allowed to spend much time with individual women. If you were interested in possibly marrying one of them you'd have to ask permission to go on what was called a 'Waiting Period' where you were allowed to spend an hour or two each day talking together. You weren't allowed to hold hands or have any other physical contact. Once you got engaged then you were allowed to hold hands; the rules were very well defined.

I wasn't supposed to have sex with my wife or even sleep in the same bed with her during her menstruation because she was 'unclean'. There were clear guidelines about what was considered godly and what wasn't. Male masturbation was out, unless you were a single brother – and then you could masturbate if you weren't thinking about any woman in the community. That was like a deadly sin. Female masturbation was totally out; women were considered to have no need for that whatsoever.

Three months after we joined the community our youngest child was born. They wouldn't allow doctors, but we had a midwife. Four weeks after the baby was born he came down with RSV bronchiolitis, which was life-threatening for a newborn.

At this stage we were still in contact with our own doctor and she said we needed to get him to hospital immediately. We told the elders and they said, 'If you want to take him to hospital we support that decision. However, if you have enough faith in God to heal your son, then we'll support that decision as well.'

All of a sudden it came down to a test of faith. I said, 'I don't have enough faith, so I'll have the car and take him to hospital.' We got him into the emergency room just as he stopped breathing. He would have died if we hadn't taken him.

Despite all that, for the first year I was happy. There were some positives but there were a lot of negatives too.

Getting rid of all of my possessions was great – it was so liberating. I never really liked having much stuff anyway. Living with a bunch of people who are really passionate about something is also a great experience. You'd never get that in any workforce – so many people working for free and really striving towards a common goal. However, the problem was – that goal was a lie. It was not a true common goal and I think people were getting duped.

It was just complete brainwashing, I was brainwashed. But at least I kept my reasoning. One thing they tell you is that you've got to give up thinking – though they don't say it in such a direct way. I have quite an analytical mind though, so I just kept a tally of all these things that didn't add up. I kept a tally of what they told me and then what actually happened.

In hindsight I was flabbergasted they were able to have such a hold over me. If you had asked me, five years ago, who would be the least likely person I knew to join a cult, I would have said me – no way would I do that. But they're very subtle; they're really lovely people and they look in your eyes and they speak with conviction, and you want to believe them. They don't tell you everything; they just tell you the good bits – they tell you what they think you want to hear.

One of my big problems with them was that I asked very specific questions relating to their being a cult, and they lied to me.

It was very oppressive for children – the discipline was horrendous. It's all based on the Bible and they give very good arguments for why it's necessary.

I'm quite ashamed that I didn't leave earlier – particularly after one incident out there. We'd only been there for a month or two at that stage. I left this man in charge of my son. He asked my son to come to him and the boy didn't, which was fairly normal three-year-old behaviour. So the man smacked him six times on the hand with a balloon stick, which is a thin bamboo rod – it's very painful.

He put my son down and asked him again to come to him – and he didn't. I asked how many times he did this to the boy, and it was about ten times and each time he hit him.

Then he told me, 'But finally the child submitted.'

I'm sick when I think about it now. But I was in a different place then. At the time I didn't know what to do – this man had been there a lot longer than I had and therefore knew more than I did.

Particular people were allowed to beat the children. If you were left in charge of a child, most times you'd be allowed to discipline them physically.

I was never aware of any sexual abuse of the children; that was one thing I couldn't have come at. However, in overseas communities of the same cult, quite a few children are bringing legal cases against the elders and others for sexually abusing them.

After the first year I started asking questions. I wanted people to tell me particular things and why they believed certain things. What I found out was that a lot of people there didn't believe in the teaching; they just went along with it. But I didn't join this group just to go along with it. I joined it because I believed in what they told me – that it was good to live with one another, to love God by loving each other and by laying down your life to do that.

It's like *Animal Farm*: everyone's equal; it's just that some are more equal than others. But it's not even close to being equal.

In November 2000 Sally and I were sent to a community in Canada to work. That was when my eyes were really opened, because this was a much older, larger community and it was quite dysfunctional. It was there that I could see the group for what it really was. After about six months there I lost all interest in the group and just started breaking myself out of it.

Sally wouldn't say a word when I expressed my concerns to her and as soon as I finished talking to her she'd go off and dob on me.

We were over there for September 11, and one of the leaders got up one day and said we had to be more like the people who flew the airplanes. Not that we should go out and kill anyone, but we should be so focused that nothing else mattered.

I said to Sally, 'That is what scares me. We cannot just be blind robots. We've been given brains and we need to use them.'

I suggested we should go home and revisit our decision based on what we now knew about the group. She went and told the elders and they kicked me out for threatening her, because I had said if she didn't come I was going to leave and take the kids with me.

It was pretty stressful. I only had $100 given to me and they dropped me and my son off at a hotel which had pornography on the front counter and signs advising guests to double-lock their doors.

I got in touch with my family; they wired me some money, and my brother came over with a plane ticket.

I still didn't realise at this stage that they were a cult; I just didn't believe in their philosophies any more.

When Sally and the other kids got back, I arranged a meeting with her. She turned up with all the kids' clothes packed – everything, even though it was just supposed to be a weekend visit.

She was still breastfeeding our youngest child at the time. When I got the baby seat out of the car I saw that she had a rod there to discipline him on the drive. This filled me with rage and, at the same time, shame for what I used to do as well.

We went for a walk while my mum looked after all the children. I tried to talk to Sally and told her why I left; I talked about our history, and she never said a word.

213

She wanted to be with the group more than with me or her children. She left without saying goodbye to the children.

I then tried to arrange visits between her and the children, but she wasn't interested. We had a few phone calls in 2002 and that's been it. I have no idea where she is now.

It would have been easier if she had died in a car accident, easier to explain to the children. It's very difficult to say that she has a mental illness and that people are lying to her. The kids are now aged eight, six and four.

Every mother must know it's not OK to just abandon their children; it's the worst thing a mother can do – particularly for my eldest daughter. She was in tears one night and said, 'Mummy must hate me.' I've been very diligent in keeping an eye on them and getting them counselling when they need it. I've now been remarried for six months and that's been really good for the kids.

I got thrown in the deep end caring for three kids, but I love it and I always had the support of my family. I just focused on the kids and enjoyed being a father. It was a relief to have my life back. I moved on.

Contacts

Have you got an amazing or compelling story you'd like to tell? We'd love to hear it, and who knows, it may end up in a book some day.

Please email your story to Michelle Hamer at:
howitfeels_641@hotmail.com

If you want to know more about our interviewees or their experiences, here are some websites and book titles that may help.

How it feels to be abducted by aliens
www.users.tpg.com.au/ufoesa/

How it feels to survive bacterial meningoccocal disease
Amanda Young Foundation
www.amandayoungfoundation.org.au

How it feels to be lost at sea
Derryl and Aileen Huff are now raising money for the coastguard and Westpac Rescue. To make a donation contact:
nelltarly@felglow.com.au

How it feels to die and come back

Read more about Ken Mullens at

http://home.iprimus.com.au/gotztass/km/nde1.htm

Contact him at graken234@bigpond.com

His self-published books are *Returned from the Other Side* and *Visions from the Other Side*.

Other books from Summersdale

EXECUTION

A GUIDE TO THE ULTIMATE PENALTY

'Essential reading for all gore junkies' *Sunday Express*

GEOFFREY ABBOTT

Execution

A Guide to the Ultimate Penalty

Geoffrey Abbott

£9.99 Pb

Execution is a gruesomely fascinating account of methods of judicial execution from around the world and through the ages, and includes such hair-raising categories as death by cannibalism, being sewn into an animal's belly and a thousand cuts.

In his own darkly humorous style, Geoffrey Abbott describes the instruments used and their effectiveness, and reveals the macabre origins of familiar phrases such as 'gone west' or 'drawn a blank', as well as the jargon of the underworld.

From the preparation of the victim to the disposal of the body, *Execution* answers all the questions you are ever likely to ask, and some you would never want to imagine.

A former Beefeater at the Tower of London, writer and TV personality **Geoffrey Abbott** has his own collection of vintage torture instruments and is the author of nineteen books including *The Executioner Always Chops Twice* and *Lipstick on the Noose*.

[REVISED AND UPDATED]

conspiracy
theories

kate tuckett

Conspiracy Theories

Kate Tuckett

£5.99 Pb

Just because you're paranoid doesn't mean they're not after you…

Worried that the world is run by a sinister cabal operating at the very highest level of government? You could just be right. Bringing together startling evidence on topics ranging from JFK to Bush, Roswell to Harry Potter, Chernobyl to the curse of the Kursk submarine and Bruce Lee's death to Space Shuttle Columbia, *Conspiracy Theories* has a cover-up for every occasion.

Taking the
Red Pill

Science, Philosophy and Religion in
THE MATRIX

edited by Glenn Yeffeth

Introduction by David Gerrold

summersdale *non fiction*

Taking the Red Pill

Science, Philosophy and Religion in The Matrix

Glenn Yeffeth

£9.99 Pb

How many layers of meaning lie in The Matrix?
'More than you will ever know.'

– The Wachowski brothers
(writers and directors of *The Matrix*)

Taking the Red Pill is a thought-provoking, mind expanding thrill ride through *The Matrix*, examining the technological challenges, religious symbolism and philosophical dilemmas the film presents. Renowned scientists, technologists, philosophers, scholars, social commentators and science fiction authors provide engaging and provocative perspectives. *Taking the Red Pill* will change how you view *The Matrix* – and the world around you.

www.summersdale.com